What people are saying abou

"Pamela Sims has breathed life into a marvelous philosophy for educating and nurturing children. *Awakening Brilliance* is a rare book that speaks to both the heart and the mind. You will revel in its insights and find a true path toward determining our future through our children."

Laurence M. Lieberman, Ed.D.,
Consultant, Author and Speaker

"An inspiring, wise and very practical book. A must for every educator, parent and student who wants to unlock the full potential of education. It teaches how to let the light of brilliance shine through. I strongly recommend that you read it."

Martin Rutte, Co-author of
Chicken Soup for the Soul at Work

"*Awakening Brilliance* is a gentle awakening to what is really happening in traditional school systems that no longer meet the needs of today's child. If every parent read this book, there truly would be a new realization about what education could and should be."

Jeannette Vos, Ed.D., Co-author of
The Learning Revolution

"Filled with valuable 'truths' about our education system. This unique book is sure to inspire teachers to bring this positive model of education into their own classrooms. The easy-to-read format makes Pamela's subject come alive."

Bobbi DePorter, President,
Learning Forum/SuperCamp
and Author of *Quantum Learning*

"An excellent hands-on resource for teachers or anyone who cares about children. Full of insightful stories and practical information for nurturing the full potential of our youth."

Richard M. Evans, Executive Director,
National Family Partnership

"Bravo! A powerful story that can change lives. Every parent should buy two – one for themselves and one for their child's teacher."

Ken Vegotsky, Parent and Author of
The Ultimate Power

"*Awakening Brilliance* should be required reading for any teacher or parent who is committed to increasing the quality of young people's lives. Pamela Sims inspires the reader with a story as well as practical advice on every page."

John Rainforth, Ph.D.,
Counselor

"This book is inspiring reading for every educator and parent who wants a better world for children. *Awakening Brilliance* is an insightful, uplifting 'wake up' call for transformation in our schools."

Brian M. Morrissey, Author of
Ultimate Learning States

"*Awakening Brilliance* is a thought-provoking introduction to the real world of life in schools. It provides both insights and hope and is highly readable."

Ronald W. Common, Ph.D.,
Professor, Faculty of Education

"A great student-centered approach with a lot of heart. Real-life and practical."

Eric Jensen, Author of *SuperTeaching*

"An entertaining story and superb teaching for us all to learn how to create the relationships that are at the center of the emerging new paradigm in education. We're adding this book to our recommended reading list!"

Sander Feinberg, Executive Director,
Enthusiasm for Learning Foundation

"An easy, quick read, for the beginning or veteran teacher, that illustrates effective teaching philosophy and practice. We can never have enough books such as this, that emphasize the importance of building student self-esteem."

Wayne Cross,
Superintendent

"Whether you went to school, are still in school, or teach school, this book will touch your heart and soul. *Awakening Brilliance* is for anyone who either takes, or wishes they could take, the risks for new learning and joyful discovery."

Reva Nelson, Speaker, former Teacher
and Author of *Risk It!*

"Many teachers understand that essentially 'we teach who we are.' For these teachers, this book will serve as a pleasant affirmation. For teachers who 'teach the curriculum' it offers strategies they can explore to convince them of the power of the hidden curriculum."

Susan M. Drake, Ph.D.,
Associate Professor, Faculty of Education

"You teach? Read the book. Do what it says… your students will love you for it!"

Yvonne Jackson, Vice-Principal

"*Awakening Brilliance* identifies many of the issues at-risk children experience during their academic careers. Pamela explores some of the unnecessary barriers to learning and successfully advocates for children. *Awakening Brilliance* is a thoughtful, timely reminder for educators and others to reawaken their commitment and compassion for children."

Sam Karani, M.Sc.,
Psycho-Educational Consultant

"To re-ignite one's passion for teaching and to affirm one's role in influencing future generations, the reading of this book is a must."

Sandra Starr, Ed.D., ADHD Researcher
and Drug-Free Program Developer

"An uplifting story that reawakened and reaffirmed my commitment to teaching."

Joanne Crossman, M.Ed.,
Teacher-Librarian

"An outstanding book for parents and teachers! Use this book to create a safe and happy environment at home and at school, and just watch your children 'awaken their brilliance.' "

Roberta Tobey,
Parent of six children

"I hope educators will read this book and rediscover how people learn and apply that understanding to empower them to teach effectively."

Karen Levy,
Youth Education Director

"A riveting read, presented with a depth of love and caring for our children. A compelling paradigm for living all of life, far beyond the classroom."

Mike Halporn, Entrepreneur

"Pamela's book is definitely a leap into the future of education. It challenges the system, but more important, ourselves as human beings. An inspiring book for all individuals embracing life and growth, a must for everyone involved in education."

Normand Deslandes,
Speaker and Life Coach

"*Awakening Brilliance* shows through a 'coaching model' ways that we can help adults learn how to take the higher road with children. The classroom is a microcosm of society. People treated with respect and warmth will create the same."

Tom Stoyan,
Canada's Sales Coach

"It's crucial for educators to use this book as a reference to increase the communication, respect and caring in their schools. Parents should read this book to become knowledgeable about the positive difference aware educators can make in their children's lives."

Danielle Holton,
Parent of three boys

"Teachers are in a position of public trust and it's refreshing to see in *Awakening Brilliance* that we can return to a system where teachers are dedicated and care about their students instead of proficiency test scores."

Dave Sneed,
Supervisor

"*Awakening Brilliance* nicely illustrates its message... there is a lot to learn from this book."

Mary Armstrong, MSW, CSW,
Social Work Psychotherapist

"An enlightening book on how to walk through life inspired instead of defeated."

Jody Stoyan,
Business Manager

"A great book about making learning exciting. This book is exciting. A must read for all."

Danniel Star,
Counselor and Speaker

Awakening Brilliance

Awakening Brilliance

How to Inspire Children to Become Successful Learners

by

Pamela Sims, M.Ed.

Bayhampton Publications
Atlanta, Georgia, U.S.A. & Toronto, Ontario, Canada

This book is part of the: **AWAKENING THE LOVE OF LEARNING SERIES™**

Printed and bound in Canada

10 9 8 7 6 5

First printing 1997. Reprinted 1998, 1999, 2000 (updated Appendix B), 2002

Library of Congress Cataloging-in-Publication Data

Sims, Pamela, date
Awakening brilliance : how to inspire children to become successful learners / by Pamela Sims.
p. cm. -- (Awakening the love of learning series)
Includes bibliographical references (p.) and index.
ISBN 0-9651126-0-8 (pbk. : alk. paper)
1. Teachers--United States--Case studies. 2. Teaching--United States--Psychological aspects--Case studies. 3. Teacher-student relationships--United States--Case studies. 4. Motivation in education--United States--Case studies. 5. Learning, Psychology of--Case studies. I. Title. II. Series.
LB1775.2.S56 1997
371.1'023--dc20 96-4775

Canadian Cataloging-in-Print Data
Sims, Pamela, date-
Awakening brilliance: how to inspire children to become successful learners

(Awakening the love of learning series)
Includes bibliographical references and index.
ISBN 1-896766-00-5

1. Teachers – Case studies. 2. Teaching – Psychological aspects – Case studies. 3. Teacher-student relationships – Case studies. 4. Motivation in education – Case studies. 5. Learning, Psychology of – Case studies. I. Title. II. Series.
LB1775.S56 1997 371.1'023 C96-930318-1

Cover Design by Susan Hoff-Szabo and Stephen Szabo
Photograph of Pamela Sims, M.Ed. by David Leyes

ATTENTION TEACHER & PARENT ORGANIZATIONS, SCHOOLS, COLLEGES AND UNIVERSITIES: This book is available at special quantity discounts for bulk purchases for educational purposes, premiums, sales promotions, fund-raising, special books or gift-giving. Booklets or excerpts can also be created to meet your specific needs. For information contact, in the U.S.: Bayhampton Publications, PMB 264, 2900 Delk Road, Suite 700, Marietta, GA 30067-5320. In Canada: 54 Mozart Crescent, Brampton, ON L6Y 2W7. Phone: (905) 455-7331, Fax: (905) 455-0207. Web site: www.bayhampton.com.

Disclaimer— Please Read This!

Dedication

This book is dedicated to all my students. I thank each and every one of you for having taught me so much.

Mission Statement

My mission in life is to help students create a better life for themselves, help them feel capable, empowered and loved. And to help educators create schools that offer students the safety and caring they need, to risk discovering their limitless potential and awaken their inner brilliance.

Pamela Sims, M.Ed.

Acknowledgments

I acknowledge with thanks all the individuals who helped with the development and production of this book.

To my brothers Joseph and Elliott, and my parents Jack and Sylvia, for your unwavering support and belief in me and this book. And to Bobbi-Lou for your patience and unconditional love during my long hours on the computer.

To author Ken Vegotsky for your consistent encouragement and invaluable advice, whose book *The Ultimate Power* helped to guide me on my creative journey.

To Dr. Jay Smink of the National Dropout Prevention Center for your kind words and support.

To my test readers and editors: Israel Ben-Ishai, Lindsay Biro, Lynne Dorfman, Karen Englander, Yvonne Jackson, Nancy Kilpatrick, Vicki Pappas, Lynn Teatro, Heidi Quiring, Vivian Quiring and Karen Welsh, thank you for your insights and suggestions.

To Marie Nicole Levesque, George Wallace, Steve Martin, Audrey Simtob, Dustin Reid and Nicole Brock for your assistance during my research project.

To Bobbi DePorter, Joe Chapon and Mark Reardon of Learning Forum-SuperCamp for the knowledge and insights imparted to me during my enlightening association with you.

To Susan Hoff-Szabo and Stephen Szabo, thank you for creating the gorgeous cover for this book and for all the time and attention to detail that you put into it.

To my nephew Brian, and my nieces Leanna and Sarah for your love and support.

To George for encouraging and helping me to "Awaken my own Brilliance."

Introduction

It is my fervent hope that *Awakening Brilliance* will be read by people all over the world who have any sort of responsibility for the education of children, or for their care.

Awakening Brilliance combines the skills of a fine storyteller/novelist with a deep sensitivity for what children need, and paces the reader so that any teacher, administrator, parent or care-giver will be able to learn, through the vicarious experience of reading, what it takes to be a "great" teacher instead of just a "good" teacher.

I particularly like the way the material is laid out. First we get the information in story form and then in an appendix that makes everything available for easy reference.

I am very much inspired by *Awakening Brilliance* and will fall back on it in many different ways as I think further about my own communication with teachers and students and how to present information so that people can best understand and use it.

Awakening Brilliance is a gift to the children of the world and to those who teach and those who care for them. It was written not just by a great teacher, but by a great soul.

Peter Kline, author of *The Everyday Genius*

Contents

Part Two: The Awakening

Foreword

This is a phenomenal book that will improve your child's life forever.

Awakening Brilliance reads like a fast-paced novel, yet the story informs and convinces us of the desperate need to change the way students are treated in the school system. It will inspire you to bring about the changes in attitude and behavior in the schools, that are necessary for children to succeed not only in school, but in life.

Unfortunately, daily, I hear about students who are turning away from school and dropping out, looking for solutions to their problems from drugs or gangs. *Awakening Brilliance* shows us how to stop this cycle of defeat by demonstrating how to build a sense of belonging and trust in the classroom.

The book offers concrete strategies to open communication and build caring, lasting relationships with students, even the difficult ones. It shows us how to create educational environments where students want to be, where they can succeed.

Pamela has done a wonderful job of weaving her experiences as a teacher and consultant into this enlightening story. It demonstrates how integral a part educators and parents play in helping children develop their feelings of self-worth. And in today's world, how children view themselves is very important, for it's these feelings of self-worth that affect how they will succeed now and in the future.

Schools are continuously looking for ways to create happier, more productive learning environments. *Awakening Brilliance* is a book that should be a part of every school's mandate for change. It will help you create schools that promote caring, responsibility and lifelong learning. It will help you develop in children the feelings of self-worth they need to "Awaken their Brilliance."

I strongly recommend that *Awakening Brilliance* be read by all new and experienced teachers, parents and students.

Dr. Jay Smink, Executive Director,
National Dropout Prevention Center

Prologue

"We do know that everyone's potential goes far beyond anything ever realized."
— Peter Kline, *The Everyday Genius*

Wouldn't it be wonderful if the joy of discovery and learning we see in very young children would continue throughout every day of each student's life?

Having a good education is very important for an individual to be successful in life. Yet many students are choosing instead to drop out, use drugs or join gangs. In this book you will find out what you can do to reverse this trend.

Awakening Brilliance is the story of a journey of discovery. It will take you from the way school often is for many students today, to the wonderful way it could be for them tomorrow. The solutions in *Awakening Brilliance* are very powerful, yet amazingly simple.

Many of the problems you will read about in this story are often accepted as a natural part of the educational process. But it's these problems that must be challenged and changed, if we want children to develop the feelings of self-worth they need to become confident, responsible, lifelong learners.

Is there a difference between a "good" teacher and a "great" teacher?

Yes, there is. A good teacher teaches students to read, write and do math. A great teacher relates to the whole student – mind, body and soul. Great teachers have the ability to be non-judgmental and caring to all the students placed in their care.

The student stories in *Awakening Brilliance* are true. The names and situations have been fictionalized to protect the students' identities.

Pamela Sims, M.Ed.

Part One

The Voyage

Chapter 1

In the Beginning

Who said change isn't possible? Jane Madison, principal of East County Elementary School, had come to believe that in life the only thing you could count on *was* change. There were people who were a part of it and people who were opposed to it. But there was always change.

Jane watched the smiling, excited faces of the students as they walked past her on their way to their next class. It was hard to believe that only a short time ago, school life was not so pleasant at East County.

Four Months Ago

Jane Madison watched from her office doorway as the fourth grade students lined up quietly outside their classroom.

The students waited anxiously while their teacher, Miss Campbell, a plump woman with gray hair, stood in front of Wesley. Slowly she lowered her face into his and bellowed, "You idiot! You must have a head of rock!" Her voice echoed down the hall.

Wesley, a robust boy of ten with cropped black hair and big brown eyes, stood pressed against the wall. He was trying to smile to maintain what little was left of his dignity.

Finally, Miss Campbell turned away from Wesley and faced the rest of the students. "And that goes for all of you too. Don't ever let me catch any of you fooling around in line again."

The students cringed.

Jane watched silently, wishing Lillian Campbell hadn't done that. Jane was new at East County. She was in her mid-thirties, conservatively dressed, her auburn hair short and stylish. This was her first assignment as principal.

East County Elementary School was one of the older schools on the outskirts of Pittsburgh. The school had seen the neighborhood change over the years. Many had moved away, leaving behind only those who dreamed of a more affluent lifestyle. The school housed students from first to seventh grade. They came from a range of ethnic backgrounds, creating a unique and interesting challenge for Jane and her teachers.

Watching Lillian Campbell triggered Jane's memory. Last week she had observed Peter Hopkins, a thirty-year veteran of the school system, teach a lesson to his second graders. Jane remembered how stuffy and cluttered his classroom was. He must have saved every piece of paper since he had begun teaching.

Peter had been moving between the rows of students asking questions and the kids had been politely putting up their hands. He looked around, smiled at little seven-year-old Sasha, and picked her. She stood up confidently and gave Peter her answer.

Jane flinched as she remembered how Peter's smile faded and how his eyes bored into Sasha as he said sarcastically, "Why did you put up your hand when you know you don't know the answer?"

Sasha slunk down into her chair. Her hand didn't go up again.

After class Jane stayed behind to talk with Peter. Sasha lingered in the room, waiting for something.

Jane gestured toward Sasha with a questioning look.

"Oh, she's always looking for attention," Peter complained. "Puts her hand up, never knows anything. I don't know why I bother with her."

Pain registered on Sasha's face. Quietly she left the room.

Sasha's mother had called that afternoon; Sasha didn't want to go to school anymore. Could Jane find out why?

Jane knew Peter didn't like Sasha. He didn't have anything good to say about any of his students. She doubted talking with him would change a thing.

Jane walked down the hall toward Lillian Campbell's room. The students were quiet. The room appeared neat and tidy. The books and learning materials were all in their proper places. The students' desks were arranged in groups of four, except for Wesley's. His desk was off by itself next to the teacher's. Jane observed Lillian hovering over Wesley.

"If you talk one more time, I'll move you right out of the classroom," Lillian threatened. "You're nothing but a troublemaker."

Jane felt a pang of remorse as Wesley looked down at his work, his spirit broken.

As Jane headed back toward her office, she overheard two teachers talking in the teachers' lounge. She stopped for a moment to listen. It sounded like Fran Lopez, the fourth grade teacher, and Jody Goldstein, from fifth grade. The two had a combined teaching experience of about seven years. Jane had liked them both immediately when she had first met them. They seemed to be vibrant, committed teachers. Fran, with short dark hair and dark eyes, had a gentle, caring manner with the kids. Jody was a smaller, quieter woman with soft brown eyes and curly blond hair. She was a good teacher, but not as self-assured as Fran.

"Did you hear about the new programs they've added to the Social Studies curriculum?" Fran asked.

"What do they want us to do now?" Jody sounded exasperated.

"I don't know. It's probably just another one of their ineffectual stabs at trying to solve the education problems."

"You'd think they'd have learned by now that if they're going to keep adding new programs, they need to take some away. There's only so much time in a day. What do they want from us? We can't do it all."

"They never think we do enough," Fran lamented. "I don't know what people expect anymore. No matter what we do, we can't seem to make anyone happy."

"Shoot! I just remembered I have a committee meeting tonight." Jody sounded like that was the last thing she wanted to attend.

"Which committee?"

"Promoting community relations with the school."

"You mean more hot dog and pizza days? I hate them."

"I do too, but we need to raise money and we need parental support to do that."

"I wish the administrators would figure out a way to balance their budgets so we wouldn't have to do all these other things, including paperwork up to our eyeballs," Fran sighed. "Then maybe we could get down to the business of actually teaching kids, like they hired us to do in the first place."

"Dream on. Those days are gone. Once you've finished disciplining half your class, the day's almost over. Who has time to teach?"

"I wish I did," Fran answered wistfully.

"Oh yeah, well I tell you, there's nothing good in this job anymore."

Jane heard a third voice join the conversation. It sounded like Peter Hopkins.

"Then why are you still teaching?" Fran asked.

"Pension. Five more years and I'm out of here. I can't wait. Kids have changed. They never used to be like this. I don't know why

I put up with all this crap anymore." Peter sounded disgusted.

Jody laughed. "Yes, you do."

"Oh yeah, my pension. I'd better not forget why I'm here."

"I guess it's just another one of those days," Jody sighed.

"Far too many for my liking," Peter stated adamantly.

Jane paused before heading back to her office. What was happening in her school? Even her newer, eager teachers were complaining about the kids, the school system, the parents and anyone else within target distance.

"I wish it were Friday." Jane overheard Jody mutter as the teachers left the teachers' lounge.

Oh great, thought Jane. *Today is only Monday.*

Jane's office was furnished with a desk, a small round conference table and a few extra chairs. An adventuresome student had skillfully carved his name in her wooden desk many years ago. His monument to himself remained to this day.

Jane sat down to finish reading the mid-term report cards. She picked up the pile from Margaret Higgins' seventh grade class.

After reading several of the reports, it seemed to Jane that Margaret's students either did really well or very poorly. "Bobby is working below grade level. He needs to pay more attention in class if he wants to pass his school year."

Jane glanced at the far wall. There was Bobby Mendez' drawing of East County Elementary School. It was wonderful the way he had captured the urban essence of the building. Bobby was a very talented artist, but he couldn't sit still in class. He was always tapping his fingers or moving his feet. He would get up to sharpen his pencil several times during his teacher's lesson. No wonder he wasn't making any academic progress.

It's strange, thought Jane. *Give that child a paintbrush and his attention never wavers. Too bad he can't transfer that same concentration to his schoolwork.*

Barbara Jones, a slender teacher with an angular face framed by shoulder-length red hair, poked her head into Jane's office. "I'm having problems with Gordon again."

"Where is he?" Jane asked.

"Sitting out here. May I speak with you first?"

"Sure, come in and close the door."

Barb walked to Jane's desk and stood facing her. "I'm totally frustrated."

"What did he do now?" Jane asked, with a sinking feeling.

"He's bullying the kids in my class again. He threatened Melissa, said he would beat her up on the way home from school. She's all upset now. You know, it never stops. These kids from the housing projects, they need to learn how to behave."

"Send him in. I'll talk to him."

Barb ignored her. "I think it's time we suspended him. Let his mother deal with him for a change. I'm tired of putting up with his antics."

"His mother works. He'd be home alone if we suspended him."

"Where's his dad?"

"He left last month. No one has heard from him since."

"Well, with a kid like that," Barb gestured toward the closed door, "would you stick around?"

Jane shrugged. "I understand what you're going through. He's been in here after almost every recess this month. He's been fighting with everyone. I'm tired of seeing him too, but he's going through a tough time."

"But he never stops. He doesn't listen. He doesn't do anything right. I don't know what to do with him anymore." Exasperated, Barb raised her hands and dropped them in frustration.

"Let me deal with him."

Barb walked to the door. "If you can't suspend him, how about an in-school suspension? That'll show the little delinquent he can't behave that way and stay in my classroom."

Barb opened the door and motioned to Gordon.

A blond, blue-eyed eight-year-old with longish, disheveled hair entered Jane's office. He was wearing a T-shirt bearing the slogan "Here comes Trouble."

Barb looked at Gordon, rolled her eyes, and left.

Gordon stared defiantly at Jane, almost daring her to punish him.

Jane raised her voice. "This is the last time I want to hear that you've threatened any of the children in this school. Do you hear me?"

Gordon pushed out his lower lip and nodded. "Yeah," he said bluntly, with no conviction.

This irritated Jane. "No recesses for a week. Now, sit outside in the reception office for the rest of the day." She dismissed Gordon with a wave of her hand.

He gave her a look as if to say, is that the best you can come up with? Then he shuffled out of her office.

She watched him leave. He could be so annoying.

Jane picked up the last batch of report cards. They were for Carole Chan's Special Education class. Carole had waited until her own children were grown before she began teaching. She had been an optimistic and vibrant forty-year-old with a mission. She had wanted to help students with learning disabilities overcome their problems. But now, after teaching for only six years, Carole complained incessantly about her students. They were always breaking the classroom rules, swearing or getting into fights. School work was the last thing on their minds.

Jane began to wonder if the negativity from her teachers was contagious. She was tired of dealing with unhappy, discontented teachers. Tired of listening to parents complain about programs, teachers and the other children. Tired of kids fighting and complaining about each other. Being the principal of a school was more difficult than she had anticipated. When she had taken over at the beginning of the school year, she had been excited about all the wonderful changes she was going to make. She had thought she could make a difference. Now, she wasn't so sure. Nothing seemed to be any different, except that she was worn out and frustrated. Thank goodness for Spring Break next week.

The ringing of her telephone brought her back to the present. It was Bill Carson, principal of East County Junior High. He was a stout, balding man in his early fifties. Jane thought of Bill as her mentor. He was wonderfully supportive and had been a great help to her at the start of the school year. He understood the district's bureaucracy and how to get what you needed from the bureaucrats.

"Hi Bill," Jane's voice lacked enthusiasm.

"You don't sound too great. What's up?" Bill asked.

"Just tired, very tired. I'm glad Spring Break is coming."

"It takes time to get this job under your belt. You're very idealistic, but change takes years. Believe me, I know. I've been doing this job for thirteen years. It's not a piece of cake. Are you getting away for the break?"

"I thought I'd head down to the Florida Keys."

"Good idea, you deserve a rest. Take it easy, have some fun while you're down there. Forget about this place. It'll still be here when you get back."

Jane wished she could take it easy. She rarely made time for leisure activities. Her work was too important to her. She was always trying to improve and change things. But now she was afraid she might have reached the limits of her ability.

She shook her head, dismayed; she didn't want to think about it. "I'll try. I'll call you when I get back."

Chapter 2

By Accident

The sun shone warmly on Jane as she dawdled along the white sandy beach. Coming to Key West had been a good idea.

She eyed the people lounging on the beach, reading or tanning, and yearned to be able to relax long enough to forget about school. She thought about what a fighter she used to be, but now she felt like all of the fight had been drained out of her.

A tall, imposing, young man in green jogging shorts approached her. "Want to go for a ride on a jet-ski? Only ten dollars."

Jane smiled and shook her head. "Maybe next time."

"Try it this time for ten dollars. My prices are going up tomorrow."

Jane looked at the jet-ski and then out at the clear, calm ocean. She had never been on a jet-ski before, but didn't want to admit it.

"Five dollars." She figured he would leave her alone.

"Okay, but just for you. Don't tell anyone."

Jane laughed. She was wearing her black and red bathing suit. "No pockets," she gestured, showing she had no money. "I guess it will have to be next time."

"You look honest, I trust you. Ten minutes for five dollars." James motioned her toward the jet-ski and began pushing it to the water.

Jane held back. Her dark brown eyes looked at the ocean, then quickly back to the beach. Her feet felt glued to the sand.

"Come on," he called, as he started the jet-ski. "Your time's ticking."

Jane slowly lifted her legs and made them move forward. Her stomach tightened, but her heart craved a new adventure. She mounted the jet-ski.

"Now remember, only ten minutes. Watch for me, I'll signal when your time's up."

Jane nodded as she revved the engine and headed out, picking up speed.

Her short hair flew in the wind. Her slim body goose-bumped as the warm breezes slid over her skin.

This is fun, thought Jane. She opened up the throttle. The sun beat down as she pointed the jet-ski straight out, away from the beach and into the open water.

Lost in the freeing sensation, all she wanted was to escape. Escape from all of her responsibilities, away from everything.

She closed her eyes and lifted her face toward the sun. The warmth invigorated her. She felt like she was being loved by the sun.

What's that noise? Jane wondered. She heard sputtering and looked around. There were no other boats near her. She pushed the throttle; nothing happened.

She looked down at her jet-ski and then all around her. She couldn't see land. The sputtering stopped. So did her jet-ski!

Okay don't panic, she thought. *That guy must be watching me. My ten minutes should be up by now, or will be very soon. He'll come looking for me. He'll save me.*

Jane scanned the empty ocean, glad she knew she would be saved; there was nothing to be afraid of.

She felt the top of her head – it was hot. *A hat,* she thought. *I should have worn a hat.* She felt the heat of the sun on her face. She licked her dry lips. Panic started to creep in. *Don't be silly, you'll be rescued shortly. Where is he?* Jane searched the clear, calm ocean.

Chapter 3

Rescued

Jane opened her eyes. A cold, wet cloth covered her forehead. She sat up abruptly and the cloth dropped to her lap. She touched the unfamiliar brass headboard to steady herself as she peered around the room.

Only a small amount of light managed to sneak through the closed venetian blinds. Seeing was awkward. An antique pine dresser, with light reflecting off the mirror above it, was all that Jane could make out.

"How are you feeling?"

Startled, Jane jerked her head around. A woman was sitting in a chair in the corner of the room.

"Where am I?"

"In my home," the woman answered.

"Where's that?"

"Don't be frightened. You were rescued from the sea and brought here."

"I don't remember being rescued."

"You were delirious from the heat."

"Delirious from the heat? You saved me?"

"You were brought here by a young friend of mine. He didn't know where else to bring you. Perhaps you should rest a while longer, then we'll have some supper."

"Oh no, I have to get back." Jane tried to stand. "I've inconvenienced you too much already."

As dizziness overtook her, Jane fell back onto the bed.

"Sunstroke is serious. Please rest."

Jane closed her eyes and put her hands to her head to stop it from spinning.

The woman stood up. "I'll be in the next room if you need me. My name is Sarah."

Jane heard Sarah leave the room. She tried to open her eyes but quickly shut them again. Her head throbbed. She was tired. But where was she? And who was this woman, Sarah?

Chapter 4

When Paths Cross

The room was almost dark. The venetian blinds blocked out what little was left of the daylight. Jane rose from the bed and unsteadily entered the next room. She heard voices. Slowly she headed through a small living room to a door that led to the outside.

Jane paused. A man, dressed in a striped blue and white T-shirt and white shorts, sat on the porch swing talking to Sarah. Sarah sat in a rocking chair. As Jane stepped onto the porch, their talking ceased.

Jane took a deep breath of ocean air. The breeze caressed her face. *What a lovely place,* she thought. A house on the ocean had always been her dream.

She gazed at the unpretentious, yet well-kept house, beautifully set back on a slight rise a few hundred feet from the ocean. The sandy beach sprawled out in front of her.

The wooden house had recently acquired a fresh coat of white paint. A garden of wild flowers and climbing roses framed the property on one side, while a vegetable garden defined the border on the other. The wooden porch looked like it had been a recent addition. On it was a white garden table holding up a colorful pink and yellow sun-umbrella. Beside the table was a swing for two and a well-worn maple rocking chair.

Jane looked out at the ocean and listened to the waves rolling slowly up onto the sandy beach. The red glow from the setting sun created a picture, almost too beautiful, almost too perfect.

Sarah stood up and approached Jane. Her long, black hair blew lightly in the breeze creating a striking contrast with the long, white, cotton caftan she was wearing. The woman's face seemed gentle, almost serene. She was not young and not old.

"Are you feeling better?" Sarah asked.

Jane nodded. "Much, thanks."

"Come. I want to introduce you to my friend Charlie. He saved your life."

Charlie stood. He was a man in his thirties with tousled hair, bleached from the sun, and a deep tan. Jane looked into his sparkling blue eyes. They were warm and disarming. She offered him her hand. "Hi, I'm Jane Madison. Thank you for saving me." Jane tried to sound more in control than she felt.

Charlie grinned as he shook her hand. "It was lucky I spotted you."

"It sure was," Jane agreed.

"Where're you from?"

"Pittsburgh. I'm a principal back there. I'm on Spring Break."

"Are you hungry?" Sarah interrupted. "You slept through supper. Shall I make you something to eat?"

Jane was about to refuse when her stomach rumbled. She laughed, slightly embarrassed, and nodded. "I'd like that."

As Jane munched on her rice, shrimp and vegetables, she listened to the lapping of the waves as they repeatedly hit the shore and retreated.

She gazed at Sarah, who was rocking gently in her rocking chair. Jane sensed a peacefulness about her that she wished she could share. But then, Jane frowned, Sarah didn't have to deal with the frustrations of being an educator.

"What happened to the jet-ski?" Jane asked.

"I took it back to James," Charlie answered. "He was very worried when you didn't return."

"I thought he would come and save me."

"He only has the one jet-ski. He's new in the business. He figures you owe him fifty-five dollars."

"Fifty-five dollars?" Jane was shocked. "I told him five!"

"Five for ten minutes. You were out there almost two hours."

"Oh my goodness!" Jane realized how lucky she was to have been rescued.

She looked down at her arms and felt a slight burning sensation beneath the robe she wore.

"I put some aloe vera oil on your skin to help soothe the burning," Sarah said. "If it starts to hurt, you may need some more."

Jane smiled gratefully and sat back, lulled into a meditative state by the ocean breezes. She closed her eyes and realized how very tired she was. Then taking a deep breath of ocean air, she slowly rose from her chair. "I really should be getting back to my hotel. Will you please call me a cab?"

"I'll drive you," Charlie offered. He reached into his pocket for his car keys.

Jane gave a tired smile of appreciation.

Sarah walked Charlie and Jane to his van. "Come again." She waved as the van pulled away.

As Jane watched the scenery go by the passenger window, she wondered out loud, "I'm not quite sure what it is about Sarah, but she seems really different." She turned to Charlie for a response.

He only nodded slightly and continued driving.

Jane sighed, leaning her head back on the headrest. "I felt so safe and secure in her home and I don't even know her."

"Sarah is a very special person. At one time she really helped me. I owe her a lot."

Jane glanced questioningly at Charlie.

"There's always a reason when two paths cross," he answered.

Chapter 5

Sarah

The next day Jane felt a lot better. Wearing a long-sleeved T-shirt, white pants and a big floppy hat to protect her sunburned face, she wandered down the beach in the opposite direction from the day before. She wanted to avoid a confrontation with James. She could have died out there in the middle of the ocean. She had no intention of giving him fifty-five dollars.

As the salty smell of the ocean breeze began to calm and relax her, Jane thought about Sarah. There was something intriguing about her. Maybe she should go back and visit her. But this time, by land.

"Hi!" Jane waved as she approached Sarah, who was crouched, weeding her small vegetable garden.

Sarah looked up and grinned, "Welcome back."

Jane smiled hesitantly. Suddenly she felt very uncomfortable. She shifted from one foot to the other.

Sarah put down her trowel and stood up, brushing the remnants of soil from her shorts and blouse; her dark eyes encouraging Jane to continue.

"Sarah, I feel like there's something I need to talk to you about, but I'm not sure what it is, or even if there *is* anything. Do you know what I mean?"

Sarah smiled. "Come in and I'll fix us some tea."

Jane followed Sarah into the house. The sun brightened up the living room, making it homey and inviting. Jane was immediately drawn to the scenic color photographs on the walls. Large framed pictures of beautiful ocean scenes, colorful sunsets, flying gulls and stranded starfish graced the walls of the living and dining areas.

"Who took these photographs? They're wonderful."

"I did," Sarah called from the kitchen.

Jane was fascinated. She wandered around the room admiring the pictures, then stopped in front of a plaque on the wall. It read "TO A GREAT TEACHER," and it was signed by hundreds of people. Some signatures looked like parents', others like kids'. Jane was engrossed in reading the names when Sarah came up behind her.

"It's from my students."

"All of the signatures? Some look like adults'."

"That's what happens to kids – they grow up. But they never forget what happened to them in school."

Jane turned to face Sarah. "You were a teacher?"

Sarah nodded as she placed the tray on the glass-topped coffee table.

Jane took a cup of tea from the tray and sat down on the rattan sofa opposite Sarah. "What made you such a great teacher?"

Sarah's face grew serious. "Do you believe you have an effect on your students' lives?"

Jane shrugged. After the last few months at school, she really wasn't sure why she had even become an educator.

Sarah set her cup down. "A few months ago I ran into one of my former students, Michael. He was vacationing here in the Keys. I hadn't seen him in years. He had been one of my third grade students, during my first year of teaching. He's all grown up now with children of his own. We spent many hours over tea, catching up on the past years. Michael has become a construction worker. He's good at his job and he loves it.

"We talked about the books I've been writing and I showed Michael my computer setup. We composed a letter to a mutual friend and I printed it out. Then I handed Michael a pen to sign the letter. He just stared at me, an embarrassed look on his face.

"'What's the matter?' I asked.

"'I... I can't write,' he said.

"'Even to sign your name?'

"He continued playing with the pen. 'I'll have to practice my signature first. I'm not used to writing it.' Michael had become very flustered.

"I was confused. 'How come?' I asked. Michael had gone from third grade to a special class for children with learning disabilities. Even though he was fairly bright, he had been experiencing a lot of difficulty in reading and had rebelled whenever he had been asked to write anything. I was astonished to learn that he'd never learned to write.

"I remember Michael was very hesitant to explain. Finally, he told me when he was in the second grade, he had a lot of problems with his printing. He said he liked to work with his hands and had always been good at building and repairing things. But when he was young he found handling small objects, like a pencil, very difficult.

"He told me that one day his second grade teacher had become so fed up with his printing that she yelled at him in front of his friends. She humiliated him so badly that he decided he would never write again, either in school or out. I remember when he told me this story, his embarrassment was so real I could see the pain in his face and hear the shame in his voice. Yet this incident happened many, many years ago. Michael has been told that he is one of the best men on the job, but they won't promote him. Why? Because he can't write."

"That's quite a story." Jane stared at Sarah.

Sarah looked sad. "Some teachers use humiliation and fear to control or motivate their students. Unfortunately, they don't realize the only thing fear and humiliation foster in children are feelings of insecurity and withdrawal. Children don't learn when they're in a state of fear."

"When I went to school my teachers taught that way," Jane admitted. "I was scared to raise my hand. I didn't want to look stupid."

"No one did, and no one does. It's human nature. We don't realize how we've been programmed to think negatively about ourselves and our abilities. I wish I had known then what I know now."

"What would you have done differently with Michael?" Jane asked.

Sarah smiled. "That's the secret to being a 'Great Teacher.'"

Chapter 6

What's Wrong with the Schools?

Sarah and Jane moved out onto the porch. Jane sat on the swing with a cup of tea in her hand, her legs tucked comfortably beneath her. The swing swayed gently as she pondered what Sarah had said. Was school supposed to be easy on kids? It hadn't been easy on her when she went to school and she had lived through it. Certainly the kids today could survive it, too.

But then again, she knew there were changes needed in the school system. Hadn't she been trying to change things at East County? Admittedly, so far, unsuccessfully, but then change takes time. Hadn't Bill said that?

"Sarah, what do you think is wrong with the way we're teaching students?"

"We're teaching curriculum instead of people," she answered simply, as she settled into her rocking chair.

"I'm not sure I understand what you mean. Teachers are supposed to teach curriculum. That's their job." Jane dropped her feet to the floor, and felt herself tensing.

"Curriculum becomes obsolete as we create it. But how students feel about themselves stays with them forever."

"Are you saying we shouldn't be teaching curriculum?"

"No. I'm saying if we don't create caring, emotionally

supportive relationships with our students first, it doesn't matter what we teach them. We'll be unable to reach them."

"Is *that* what you mean by teaching people?" The edge in Jane's voice betrayed her rejection of the idea.

Sarah nodded. "Every time teachers interact with their students, they are subconsciously programming them how to feel about themselves."

Jane narrowed her eyes. Her body remained rigid.

"It's habitual thinking. Most teachers aren't even aware they're doing it," Sarah added. "When I was teaching a Special Education class of 'slow learners,' there was a seven-year-old girl, named Karen, in my class. One day I met Karen's former first grade teacher at a meeting. She was the one who had recommended Karen for Special Education. She asked about Karen and wanted to know if she had ever learned to read. I told her not only had she learned to read, but she loved reading and spent most of her spare time with her nose buried in a book.

"Her first grade teacher was surprised. I remember she shook her head and said, 'I never thought Karen would learn to read.'

"I invited her to come and visit Karen in my classroom. She said she would call to confirm.

"The next day I told Karen that I'd met her first grade teacher, but before I could continue, she stared at me angrily and said, 'I hate her! I hate her! She always put me in the corner and told me to color. She never let me do any of the work the other kids did.'

"Karen was just seven years old and considered to be a slow learner, but she knew that teacher didn't think much of her abilities. After that, I was worried the teacher might actually show up, but she never even called."

"But," Jane interjected, "students learn even if they don't like their teachers. I did."

"How did your teachers make you feel inside?" Sarah asked gently.

Jane's eyes looked up to the right and then to the left as she searched her memory. Then, as if releasing the memory from her body, she exhaled deeply. "Not great," she admitted, putting her hand on her stomach as if she could still feel the discomfort in her body.

"Kids know what their teachers expect from them. They can feel how much they respect and care about them. But many teachers are unaware of the impact they're having on their students emotionally. They see their job as only being a teacher of reading, writing and arithmetic, rather than being a teacher of the whole person. Before teaching skills, teachers need to create a positive rapport with their students, one that inspires students to have confidence in themselves and their teachers. Then students will be able to focus their attention on learning. Without this rapport, a student's ability to learn is decreased."

Jane sat back on the swing.

Sarah asked, "How many failure messages do you think the students in your school receive every day? One? Five? Ten? Are there some of your students who get more than ten?"

Jane shifted uncomfortably in her seat, her eyes avoiding Sarah's.

"Students," Sarah continued, "who receive failure messages are being programmed to think of themselves as failures, and are afraid to risk learning, so it doesn't matter what we teach them. They'll have such a fear of failing, they won't even try. They start on a downward spiral, fulfilling the teacher's expectation of their failure."

Jane thought about Wesley and Sasha back at East County being humiliated in front of their classmates. She shuddered to think how many more students at her school were receiving the same failure messages.

Chapter 7

My Favorite Teacher

Sarah picked up her camera and invited Jane to join her for a walk on the beach. Jane declined, deciding instead to remain on the porch out of the sun.

The waves gently surfed onto the shore. The sun's rays glittered and sparkled as they danced off the clear, blue water. Sighing at the beauty of the scene, Jane gingerly sat her sunburned body down on the porch step.

Sarah returned shortly and sat in her rocking chair. After a few moments of reflection, she asked, "Who was your favorite teacher?"

"That's easy! Miss Alexander, seventh grade," Jane answered without hesitation.

"Why did you like her so much?"

"Because she liked me." Jane absentmindedly played with the sand beside the step. "She thought I was so smart. It felt good just to be around her. She was great. That's why I wanted to become a teacher, to be like her."

"When you went to school, was it important for you to feel loved and cared for?"

"If I thought the teacher didn't like me, I felt stupid. I mean, I knew I really wasn't, but I didn't feel good about anything I did."

"If it was important for you to feel loved and cared for when you went to school, do you think it's important for your students?"

Jane stared at Sarah. She was stunned. "You know, I would have done anything for Miss Alexander, just because I knew she cared about me."

Sarah leaned back in her rocker. "At one school where I was the teacher-in-charge, the eighth grade teacher sent one of her students, Gary, to see me. He was disturbing the class. Gary was the leader of the district gang."

"I hate being in situations like that," Jane interjected. "I'm always afraid of what they might do. So I just suspend them, get them out of the school."

Sarah nodded understandingly, "I thought of punishing him, but instead Gary and I sat down and talked. I found out that a lot of the anger he had brought to school that day had nothing to do with his classroom or his teacher, but with a fight he had had with his mother that morning. The fight was weighing heavily on his mind. He admitted it was keeping him from being able to concentrate on his work.

"We talked for about an hour before Gary went back to his classroom. I was totally drained and realized why it would've been so much easier to just discipline him than to take the time to really understand his problem. I could have punished Gary in two minutes and gone on my way. However, our conversation gave me a tremendous insight into how our lack of communication with students is setting them up for failure. Punishing Gary would not have changed his behavior; his behavior was only a symptom of the real problem."

"Did talking to him make a difference?" Jane asked.

"I didn't know until several weeks later when I was asked to take over that same eighth grade class. The students saw this as a wonderful opportunity to misbehave. To my surprise, before I could say anything, Gary stood up in front of the class and said, 'No, not her.

She's all right. Leave her alone.' The students immediately went back to their work.

"Did my conversation with Gary make a difference? You bet it did. We may not have solved his problems, but he knew I cared about him and that made a difference to him. He was a greatly troubled student, but I never had any problems with him. From that day onward, he would do anything for me."

Jane grimaced. "And I would have suspended him."

"It's habitual thinking. Once we understand the ways we've been taught to respond, we can change the way we do things. Part of it is realizing that punishing is not always the best way to handle things. Sometimes understanding goes a lot further."

"I guess I'm too strict." Jane admonished herself.

"Kids don't mind a teacher who's strict."

"No?"

Sarah shook her head. "Discipline is never the issue. Kids don't care if you discipline them, just as long as you care about them."

Habitual thinking. Jane had known that there was a need for change in her school. Now she was beginning to understand just what those changes might be.

Chapter 8

Confrontation

The next day Jane dawdled over lunch in the crowded outdoor cafe of her hotel. The cafe was on a patio facing the ocean and was filled with scantily-clad sunbathers. Jane looked out of place in her long-sleeved shirt, ankle-length skirt and new wide-brimmed hat that covered most of her face.

Jane stared enviously at the sunbathers. But she knew the oil Sarah had given her was the only thing keeping her skin from drying up and peeling. She was glad she wasn't an egg – she felt like her shell could easily crack open, and she'd fall out. She adjusted the umbrella on her table. She wanted protection from the hot noonday sun.

She wondered what to do today. Should she snorkel, try scuba diving or go and visit Sarah? She sipped her coffee, lost in thought.

"Ma'am."

Jane looked up and involuntarily cringed. It was James! She did not want to talk to him.

Without an invitation, he sat down at her table.

Jane noticed his T-shirt with "No Problem" written across the front. *No problem,* she thought. *Isn't that ironic.*

"Ma'am, I believe you owe me some money. I trusted you. I gave you a cheap rate and you took my jet-ski away for the whole day. I couldn't make any money. You owe me fifty-five dollars for the one hour and fifty minutes you used my jet-ski."

Jane put down her coffee cup. "Is the gas included in the price?" she asked sarcastically.

"Look, Ma'am, those things happen. It couldn't be helped. We all run out of gas sometimes."

"I almost died out there. You didn't even try to rescue me." She attempted to keep her voice calm.

"It's a big ocean. How was I supposed to know where you were? I didn't know you needed help."

"Well I did. You sent me out there without any gas." She struggled to control her anger.

"Ma'am, you had enough gas for ten minutes," James insisted.

Jane looked away. She *had* lost track of time. He could be right. But damn it, she had almost died because of him. Was she now expected to pay him for the experience?

"Ma'am, I trusted you," James said earnestly.

"Stop with the Ma'ams. My name is Jane." Frustrated, she looked out at the ocean and wished she knew what she should do – pay him or tell him to get lost?

Then slowly Jane turned her gaze back to James. Or, she thought, *is this one of those habitual situations where maybe there was a better way of handling things than embarrassing him into going away?* He didn't seem like such a bad guy. Maybe, just maybe, she would try another approach.

"James," she started, "I felt let down by you. I trusted I would be safe going out on your jet-ski. I was afraid at first, but you filled me with a feeling of excitement. Then, I almost died out there." She pushed up her sleeve to show him her burn.

James stared at her arm, then at her face, his eyes sizing up the situation. Finally he answered, "Ma'am, I mean Jane, I'm new at this game… I'm sorry. I… I needed the five to put gas in the machine." He stood up. "For you, anytime you want you can ride my jet-ski for nothing."

Jane laughed. "Not on your life! I'm not going out there again."

"But you must," James insisted, "if something makes you afraid, you have to try it right away or you'll never do it again."

"Like getting back on a horse after you've fallen off?"

James nodded, as if unsure he had been that profound, but it sounded good.

"Okay, I have an idea," Jane said, "I'd like to go and visit Sarah today. Will you take me?"

James smiled. "My pleasure to be of service to you. Just tell me when."

Jane looked down at her empty coffee cup and stood up. "How about now?"

James grabbed her hand and started jogging toward the beach, with Jane right behind him.

Chapter 9

No More Habitual Thinking

Jane burst into Sarah's house, followed by James. Her clothes and hair were disheveled from the ride on the jet-ski. "Sarah, does habitual thinking mean it doesn't come from your heart?" she called.

Sarah came out of the kitchen. "You're a fast learner."

"Oh Sarah," Jane continued excitedly, "I thought about everything you said yesterday. I realized I've been programmed all my life to think and react in ways I don't even question. Take James here." Jane smiled at James who looked unsure as to what all the excitement was about. "I realized I only knew two ways of dealing with him – get angry, or give in. I thought maybe there's another way, so I just said what was in my heart, and it worked. There was no confrontation, no anger. He understood how I felt. James drove me here on the jet-ski. Can you believe that?"

Sarah smiled broadly and said simply, "Yes."

"There's so much I want to learn from you, but there's so little time."

"You have your whole lifetime to learn, adapt and expand on what I'm sharing with you now."

Jane took a deep breath and exhaled slowly. "You make it all sound so simple."

"But it is. I'll get us some cold drinks and let's sit outside on the porch, then we'll continue."

James sat down on the sand, took off his T-shirt and turned his face toward the sun.

Jane watched him from the porch swing. Sarah had told her he was the eighth of ten children. He had quit school after tenth grade, saying it wasn't for him. He didn't seem slow; he seemed to have an innate intelligence.

Sarah leaned toward Jane, and as if she could read her mind, said quietly, "Go ahead and ask him."

Jane hesitated a moment. "James?"

He turned toward her.

"Would you mind telling me a little about yourself?"

James seemed reticent.

"Tell Jane why you left school," Sarah urged.

James' face turned red. He looked toward Sarah and shrugged. "I don't know." He looked down, embarrassed.

"Never mind, it's okay." Jane tried to save the situation.

Sarah turned to James and said gently, "Please tell her your story. She's a principal. Maybe she can prevent it from happening to someone else."

James' face held a look of uncertainty as he looked first at Sarah, then at Jane. Finally he nodded. "You're right. It's important she knows."

James took a deep breath to compose himself. "I used to live with my father, stepmother, stepbrothers, stepsisters and all kinds of different boarders who were always moving in and out of our house. I had lots of problems with my brothers and sisters. And my dad, well, he drank, and so did my stepmom. But I didn't care, I had a dream. I wanted to be a teacher, a good one just like Sarah here, and I worked hard in school. My grades were good. I was going to be the best.

"When I got to high school, I couldn't deal with my family anymore. I felt like no one cared about me. My buddies and I, we started doing drugs. Well, one day I got caught smoking marijuana in the school washroom and they expelled me."

"I'm sorry to hear that...," Jane began.

Sarah put up her hand, signaling that Jane should let James continue.

"My dad, he kicked me out and I ended up moving in with my mom, but it didn't work out either. She's an alcoholic too. I moved out on my own and went on welfare for a while. I even got married, but that was no good. I know I made a mistake doing drugs, but now I've got nothing. I could've been a great teacher, you know. All I needed was for somebody to care about me."

Sarah added, "Many students arrive at school with their emotional and physical needs unmet. When a school reacts to students' negative behavior by forcing them out of school rather than by offering them help, the long-term effects can be devastating. School may be the only safe and caring place they have in their lives, the only place where they can learn how to be successful. By not helping these students, we are doing damage, not only to them, but to society as well."

Jane's brow creased as she listened to Sarah explain.

"Some children are being left on their own, or with strangers for the largest part of their waking hours. It's from these strangers that they get their values, their goals, their dreams. It's from these strangers that they discover their self-worth and learn how to build relationships. Since we, as teachers, are the strangers who are with these children for the largest part of their day, it has become up to us to help our students feel loved and valued. If we don't help our students feel safe and happy in school while learning the skills for a productive future, our kids will go looking for happiness elsewhere, sometimes from drugs or gangs."

"But," Jane objected, "that's putting a heavy burden on the school. Parents are the ones ultimately responsible for their children's behavior, not us. We can't do everything."

"I am not saying that parents shouldn't be responsible for their children," Sarah responded. "A parent's relationship with their child is very important. And as a teacher, if you're having difficulty with a child, a parent can be your best ally. They often know their child best and, by working together, parents and teachers can help the student overcome many problems."

"Yeah, but it doesn't always work that way," James interjected. "My dad never met any of my teachers. He didn't want anything to do with the school. He said he had better things to do with his time."

Sarah added, "If the student's parents are unable or unwilling to work with the school on the child's behalf, we must make sure that we're not neglecting that student too. We may not be able to fix what's going on in their homes, but we must make sure we're not adding to their problems."

"But how do we help these kids when their behavior is usually so disruptive?" Jane asked.

James answered, "You know the guys with a bad attitude, it's because they're hurting inside. I know. I was one of them. People thought we were bad guys, bullies. They should've known how scared we were that someone would take us up on our threats."

"What should the school have done?" Jane asked.

"I needed someone to care about me, not yell and scream at me. I needed someone to help me. But I didn't know how to ask for it, or even what to ask for. Punishments only made me worse. It just told me I was right, that the world was a rotten place."

Jane felt sad. James had been so misunderstood by his school.

He wasn't bad, he was needy. He had needed his teachers to reach out to him and the school had expelled him instead.

Sarah noticed Jane's expression. "When schools fail children, those children often become a bigger problem to society."

James nodded. "I know a lot of guys who are still on drugs, or in jail. They never did get their lives back on track after being kicked out of school."

"School can be a place for teaching students how to be successful, or for adding to society's problems by confirming their feelings of inadequacy and failure," Sarah said.

Jane thought about Gordon at East County and remembered how negatively she had reacted to him. His dad had moved out. He probably felt abandoned and scared, and what did she do? She punished him. Jane let out a discouraged sigh.

Sarah stood up and reassuringly touched Jane on the shoulder. Then she picked up her camera. "Let's go for a walk on the beach before the sun goes down and we lose all the light."

The tide rushed in, flowing across their feet as the three of them strolled leisurely by the water's edge.

"Sarah," Jane broke the silence, "it's all about treating your students as you would've liked to have been treated yourself, isn't it?"

Sarah nodded. "Respect and care about them. It's really that simple."

Chapter 10

Building Self-Esteem

As Jane, Sarah and James continued their stroll, Jane asked, "How can teachers build self-esteem in their students?"

"First, by not taking it away," James answered.

Sarah laughed. "Good point. Kids usually start school excited about learning, eager to make new friends, only to end up leaving school early, or otherwise feeling disillusioned, humiliated, alone."

Jane grimaced. She knew it was true.

"When we're young," Sarah continued, "we learn how worthy we are from our parents, our teachers, our friends. The idea of being a failure doesn't cross the minds of most children until someone plants the idea in their heads. Unfortunately, teachers often give out negative comparison messages that tell students they don't measure up. Children quickly learn that no matter how hard they try, they can never be the best."

"But we're supposed to be preparing students for the real world, aren't we?" Jane asked.

James frowned, "What good is school doing, if the kids leave school feeling dumb and discouraged?"

"Some students, once they're out of school, go on to accomplish great things," Jane pointed out.

"If they feel dumb in school, then find out in the real world they're really okay, where's the reality of what's going on in school?"

James asked. "What I never understood was why I had to go to school, when all I ever got was put-downs. Did teachers think that if they kept telling me I was a loser, it would help me do better in life?"

"I guess the question we should be asking is, are teachers preparing students for real life or has school become the end in itself?" Jane queried.

"That's a good question. Because if students are leaving school with limiting beliefs about themselves, beliefs they can't dispel, most of them are bound for failure," Sarah added.

Jane looked thoughtfully at Sarah. "What can we do to change those messages?"

"Students need to feel special. Remember how you felt with Miss Alexander. What do you remember learning in her classroom?"

Jane thought for a moment and shrugged, "I don't remember much really."

"Why was she your favorite teacher?"

"She expected great things from me. She cared about me. I don't remember what she taught me, I only remember the good feelings I had in her classroom."

"So, you mean it's not what we learned, but who we learned it from that's important?" Sarah asked.

"I guess so. My grades went up that year. She helped me get those good grades. I just felt good being there."

"Were you comfortable taking risks in her class?" Sarah asked.

"With her, I could try anything. I knew she would never yell at me or put me down, even if I made a mistake… I remember I worked hard in her class. I wanted her to be proud of me. But you know, that year, everyone did well in her class. I was at a class reunion ten years later and I couldn't believe it – every student thought they had been Miss Alexander's favorite."

"What a wonderful teacher!" James exclaimed.

"She was," reflected Jane. "I guess she knew how important it was for her students to know she believed in them and cared about them. In her class I felt like I belonged, that I could be anything or do anything I wanted."

Sarah nodded. "She knew that children who aren't afraid to fail, do better in school. But if you want to build self-esteem in students, they not only need to feel safe and cared for, but they also need to feel a social connection with their peers. You know, it's strange…"

"What's strange?" Jane asked.

"Teachers know they need this connection with other teachers, but they often don't allow their students the chance to experience those same feelings with other students."

"What do you mean?"

"When teachers walk into a staff meeting, who do they sit beside?"

"Their friends, of course."

"Right. We always sit beside people who like us and avoid the people who don't. But we don't allow students the same rights. Teachers are always moving students away from their friends to discourage socializing. Yet, it's important for students to feel connected with their peers."

"So," Jane concluded, "to build self-esteem, students need to be in an emotionally safe learning environment, with people they feel a connection with."

Sarah nodded.

Jane thought of Wesley, the student in Miss Campbell's class, sitting all by himself. She felt a knot in her stomach. She knew Sarah was right.

Chapter 11

How Can I Change Things?

Jane sat across from Sarah at breakfast, savoring every bite of the eggs benedict Sarah had prepared. They were delicious.

After breakfast Jane perched herself on the porch swing. The cool ocean breeze brushed against her face, a welcome relief from the morning heat. She felt blessed being here with Sarah.

Sarah settled into her rocking chair with her second cup of coffee.

"Sarah," Jane broke the silence, "I have learned not to judge students and to work from my heart. I've learned that the anger we exhibit can limit a student's growth forever and that caring, not discipline, is the issue. But I haven't yet learned how to change what's going on in my school. I understand all the things we've talked about. You're right. They're common occurrences. We do them automatically and think nothing of it. But what can I do to create teacher-student harmony? What can I do to change things at East County?"

A smile played at the corners of Sarah's mouth. "Did you have many friends when you went to school?"

Jane thought about it. "Some."

"Did you feel different from the other kids?"

"I sometimes felt as if I didn't belong."

"Do you know, you weren't different?"

"What do you mean?"

"Many kids feel that way."

Jane looked surprised.

"Let me tell you about the 'class from hell.' I was taking over an Intermediate Learning Disabilities class for a few days while the teacher was away. The class had sixteen students in it from sixth to eighth grade. The functioning level of these students was low, and their behavior abominable. They had a drill sergeant for a teacher's assistant who frightened even me when she spoke. She decided to ignore me completely and continued to carry on the program in the classroom as if I weren't there. She held a tight rein on the students. There was no getting away with anything.

"After watching this for the first period, I couldn't take it anymore. I couldn't stand being in a classroom with that kind of atmosphere. I told her nicely that I would take over. She looked at me condescendingly, as if to say, 'You think you can handle these kids? Well then, go ahead. I was just trying to save you a lot of trouble.' I remember wanting to respond, 'If I don't, you might have to send me to the principal.'

"I invited the students to bring their chairs and sit in a semi-circle around me. I took out a picture of my dog, Sheba, and proceeded to tell them about my experiences with her. They listened carefully, and then asked me questions about my life. I then gave each student a turn to tell the class something about themselves. The kids listened intently and asked the simplest questions about each other. It was February, the class had been together for six months, yet none of them knew anything about their classmates.

"I learned volumes about these students in that short period of time. Volumes that helped me to understand and empathize with each and every one of them. Sharing helped me to appreciate where they were coming from emotionally, their home situations, their feelings and their needs. It helped me to relate to each student as a unique individual. I began to understand who they were and what they needed from me.

"The students started to respond wonderfully to me. The drill sergeant was put out to pasture. The kids were happy to cooperate and learn. They didn't need to be tightly controlled because I was meeting their emotional needs. I loved that class. I enjoyed spending time with them and they never gave me any trouble. They knew I cared about them."

"You mean just talking to the kids about your dog changed their behavior?" Jane was skeptical. "I had a cat once, but I never told any of my students about him."

"It wasn't sharing about my dog that was important; it was that I was sharing a piece of myself. I opened myself up to them and they, in turn, opened themselves up to me. Children misbehave because they're in pain. How can we, as teachers, help alleviate their pain, if we don't know what's going on in their lives that's important to them?"

Jane listened dubiously.

Sarah continued, "Teachers who spend the first part of every day sharing and caring create wonderful bonds with their students. They gain a tremendous insight into each other's lives. These insights help students feel they're not different, not alone. Students begin to feel a connection with their teachers and classmates. They feel a sense of belonging, of being accepted for themselves."

"What if a student comes into the classroom angry and disrupts the program?"

"Use the sharing time to discuss and deal with the problem. Also, the sharing time may help you to become aware of other students who may not be emotionally ready to learn. If you're unaware, making demands on some of these students may result in what seems like an irrational blowup. Not every day is a great day for learning. Teachers may have to allow students days off, too, but in a supportive way that lets them keep their dignity and permits the rest of the class to carry on with the program."

"What about the quiet ones? The ones who keep to themselves a lot. I can't see them participating."

"Reaching out and including the loners is essential," Sarah answered. "It's as important to understand the quiet, compliant student as it is to understand the boisterous one. It may take longer for the quiet ones to get used to the sharing process, but hearing how other students feel is important for them. It allows them to feel less different, less isolated."

"What if the teacher is having a bad day?"

"Share that information with the students instead of screaming at them. It gives the students a chance to empathize and identify with their teacher. They may want to make helpful suggestions, perhaps let the teacher know they care, or they may just need to know to respect the teacher's space that day. It's a very important skill students need to learn. It's teaching by modeling the behavior you want your students to copy."

"But can't sharing be scary? I don't know if I would want everyone to know what I'm really like. Especially when I'm hurting. I prefer to hide, and lick my wounds."

"Sharing at times when we wish we could become invisible isn't always easy. Sometimes when we feel hurt, we would rather strike out and hurt someone else. Unfortunately, we usually strike out at someone we love. But it's at those times it's most important for us to share, to reaffirm our self-worth, to know people care about us, to know we're still lovable. No matter what's happening in our lives."

"You know, that would feel nice," Jane agreed.

"Think of how students would feel if every morning they were greeted warmly with a smile. If the teacher asked how they were feeling, and really cared about the answer."

"I know even I would like that."

Sarah smiled. "Sharing can be magical. It means allowing people to see and accept you for who you are, the real you. And that's the greatest feeling of all."

Later that day, Jane and Sarah wandered down the beach collecting interesting-looking seashells.

Jane thought about all the negative comments students and parents had made to her about the school system. She remembered them telling her how they had felt put down, humiliated, disapproved of, discouraged, alone. *Not exactly a good formula for building self-esteem,* Jane thought.

"We really haven't done a very good job of helping students feel accepted and good about themselves," Jane said.

"It's sad," Sarah agreed. "That's why so many students are looking for those feelings of approval and belonging elsewhere."

"You mean from gangs?"

Sarah nodded. "The gang gives them a sense of belonging, of family, of power in their lives. In school, they feel they have no control over what's happening to them."

As they walked on, Jane thought, change may take time, but there really wasn't much time. Educators and society were losing the battle.

Chapter 12

How Important are Learning Styles?

The next afternoon Jane rushed through the hotel's busy lobby to the Patio Cafe. She was late for her lunch with Sarah.

Jane spotted Sarah waiting by the hotel pool, wearing a one-piece black bathing suit, her long black hair tied up in a knot. She waved to Sarah and made her way past the people standing in line for the lunch buffet.

"The water in the pool looks wonderful. Shall we have a swim before lunch?" Sarah suggested.

"Sure," Jane readily agreed and pulled her T-shirt over her head and slipped off her slacks revealing the two-piece bathing suit she wore underneath. She tossed her clothes onto the chair next to Sarah and dove into the pool.

Sarah entered more cautiously, getting used to the water with each step.

After doing several laps, Jane swam up to Sarah, who had managed to commandeer an air mattress from the pool attendant. She was floating leisurely on her stomach.

As Jane treaded water beside Sarah, her head filled with questions. There was so much more she wanted to learn from her. She asked, "Have you ever noticed how some children will do really well in school one year and very poorly the next?"

Sarah nodded. “As adults, we’re very lucky; we can choose our teachers and mentors.”

“You mean, like my being here with you?”

“Yes. But, unfortunately, children aren’t so lucky. They don’t get to choose their teachers. If they did, we might see better pupil-teacher matches.”

“I never thought of that.” Jane dove underwater and resurfaced a few feet away, then paddled back toward Sarah and continued, “The pupil-teacher match is very important, isn’t it?”

Sarah nodded. “It is, if we want students to have a successful year.”

“What would you base the match on?”

“Teaching and learning style; making sure the teacher accommodates the way the child needs to learn.”

“What if the teacher isn’t comfortable teaching that way?”

“It’s the teachers’ job to adjust their teaching style to the way their students learn, not the other way around. Teachers who don’t could be creating learning-disabled students.”

Jane was pensive. She thought of several students at East County who had learning problems.

“Unfortunately,” Sarah continued, “most students see their inability to learn as *their* fault, not as a problem with the teacher.”

“You mean teachers are creating failures and blaming the students?”

“It does happen. It’s unfortunate some teachers believe that if they know their subject, any failure by the student is the student’s problem. But if teachers can’t transfer the information from their brains to their students’ brains, their knowledge is useless.”

“I make sure my teachers are using the most up-to-date teaching techniques.”

“It’s not whether the teachers are using the latest approaches that matters, but whether or not their students can learn from that approach. There's no universal technique that works for all students. If teachers want learning to take place, they need to observe and adapt their teaching styles to the individual needs of their students." Sarah pointed toward the lunch buffet beside the pool. "Shall we?"

Jane nodded. Sarah slid off the air mattress and paddled to the edge of the pool with her.

After drying off with towels supplied by the hotel, Jane quickly put on her T-shirt and slacks. Her skin had started to peel from the sunburn and was still very sensitive to the sun. Sarah, who had pulled a light blue embroidered caftan over her head, re-tied her wet hair back with a barrette. Then they headed toward the buffet table and filled their plates with salad and fruit.

Once comfortably seated at their table, Sarah continued, "When I was teaching a Special Education remedial program, a boy from the first grade was referred to me. Mitchell was smart, but he couldn't read. He was being assessed by the school psychologist, but even before the assessment results were in, I began working with him.

"The psychologist wrote that Mitchell was a bright child and a non-reader, which had been self-evident at the time of the testing. The report recommended that Mitchell be placed in a Special Education class. I invited the psychologist in to see Mitchell, and asked the boy to read for her. In the short space of three weeks, the time it took to produce the psychology report, Mitchell was reading and loving it. He was so proud of himself."

"How did you teach him?" Jane asked.

"It was really very simple. After talking with him, I realized he was able to take in information and remember it when it was presented auditorily, through his ears. So, before Mitchell attempted to read a story, I had him learn his new words on a language master."

"Language master?"

"The language master is a machine that gives students a chance to learn reading words by themselves. The words are written on a special card. The student first tries to read the word, then puts the card into the machine. The machine says the word that has been prerecorded by the teacher and the student can hear if the word has been read correctly. Students can practice their words as often as they please and get immediate reinforcement. With this machine, Mitchell was able to see the words and repeat the words out loud to hear them, through his own ears, as many times as he needed to."

"That's all it took?" Jane was surprised.

"For him, yes. His classroom teacher was only using a pencil and paper approach. It didn't match the way Mitchell needed to learn. He needed to learn through his ears. Now there's even computer software that can be programmed to do a job similar to a language master. It allows students to get immediate auditory feedback and assists teachers in keeping track of their students' progress."

"Sounds good, but how can you tell how a child will learn best?"

"Identifying a student's learning style is important, but I found the most successful way to teach is to involve all of the children's senses during a lesson. That way you make sure there's something in each lesson that meets every child's learning needs. You don't miss anyone. Students may be strong in one sense or modality and weak in the others, but they need to develop all of their senses."

"What kinds of things did you do?" Jane asked.

"The students would talk about the work, use the language master, tape recorder, films, and video tapes to enhance the hearing part of the program. Written materials, the computer and books were used for the visual part. To help those who preferred learning kinesthetically, movement was added to the program: tracing, acting, manipulating, building, role-playing. Anything to help the students learn the information through their bodies."

"Some children need to move to learn?"

"Some do."

"And when we force them to sit still...?"

"They become restless very quickly. They're the kids who are always tapping something or moving in their seats. They're the ones often thought of as behavior problems. Kinesthetic learners don't usually do well in school, even though they may be bright. School was not designed for their movement-style of learning."

"What happens to them?"

"A lot of them end up in Special Education, some drop out thinking they can't learn. It depends. Some are self-motivated enough to succeed in spite of all the negative messages they were taught about themselves in school."

"It must have felt good, knowing you kept Mitchell from being placed in a special class."

Sarah stood up. "No, I didn't."

"What happened?"

"Ask James Ysseldyke." Sarah went to refill her plate.

Chapter 13

Politics and Special Education

"Who's James Ysseldyke?" Jane asked when Sarah returned, accepting the offer of a slice of watermelon from Sarah's plate.

"He wrote the research article, 'Declaring Students Eligible for Learning Disabilities Services: Why Bother with the Data?' "

"Why bother with the data? That's what we use to place students!"

"Unfortunately, politics may play more of a part in who gets what and when. Ysseldyke found it really didn't matter what information was presented. In fact, more than half the students declared learning-disabled had test scores showing normal or average performance."

"That's awful."

"Especially awful for the child who suffers from being labeled. If you had been diagnosed learning-disabled in school, how far would you have gone academically, or in life? If you have the chance, talk to some of the young adults who went through school labeled. You can feel their anger at having had their abilities capped and their teachers' expectations lessened. A lot of them have become lost souls."

"Like me." Charlie appeared out of nowhere dressed in a dark blue T-shirt and jeans. His plate was filled to the brim with food.

Jane felt her face light up. "Charlie, it's good to see you again."

Sarah rose and gave him a hug, careful not to upset his plate.

"I see you've fully recovered." Charlie eyed Jane with an infectious grin.

Jane smiled broadly and nodded.

"I'm glad you're okay," he added.

"I'm glad you saved me."

"Will you join us?" Sarah pulled out the extra chair.

"Sure."

"Actually, Charlie, I was just explaining to Jane about special education graduates..."

He frowned. "Yeah, I was one of them."

"You?" Jane was surprised.

Charlie laughed. "Yeah me. I guess you can call it graduation. It was all such a farce. I had problems in math and reading and it was as if that meant I was stupid. I was one of the best athletes in the school and that was okay, but people just didn't understand that I couldn't sit still. It was only after I met Sarah here, and she explained how I needed to move to learn, that I finally understood I wasn't dumb. Teachers taught *at me.* They thought it was great when I was out winning a football game for the school, but they didn't take the time to understand what I needed from them."

"That's sad," Jane acknowledged.

"What's even sadder," Sarah added, "is that when I met Charlie, he had such a low opinion of himself."

"You?" Jane couldn't believe it.

Charlie nodded.

"Since Charlie left school, he's become a very successful businessman," Sarah explained. "He has a sailing and scuba diving school, and a store that sells everything for water sports. It's the best in the Florida Keys. Yet once, he was embarrassed to tell me that he had failed tenth grade math three times. I told him if you can count to a million, who cares?"

Jane laughed.

"You know," Charlie said, "since leaving school, I've come to believe that what schools think of as normal is too narrow. We don't allow for people with different abilities to be grouped under normal."

Sarah grinned. "You can tell he's one of my students. He now understands how he was taught to feel negatively about himself because he didn't learn in the same way as the other students."

"She's right," Charlie said. "All those poor report cards – I thought I was dumb, especially compared to all the kids who were good at school work. From Sarah I learned to honor my own uniqueness. I'm okay just the way I am."

"We have to broaden our understanding of the range of normal," Sarah added, "to include the different ways people learn. So often, it's a mismatch of learning and teaching style, not intelligence, that determines how well or poorly a child is learning. Look at Charlie, a perfectly intelligent 'normal' human being, who was declared learning-disabled because he's a kinesthetic learner."

Charlie nodded. "I never sit still. The more I move, the more I learn. But you know what? I think we judge kids too much by what they can't do, rather than by what they can do. Many teachers don't understand that a disability in school may not be a disadvantage in life. I'm living proof of that."

"With the present definitions of normal, we could all be labeled learning-disabled," Sarah stated.

"But why does a student have to be labeled 'disabled' to get the extra help they need?" Charlie asked.

"It's the way we keep track of students," Jane answered.

"But it's so emotionally damaging. I should know. I can't believe schools go that route when all the research for the last fifty years has said, 'Don't label!'"

Jane looked at Sarah. "How can we do it differently?"

"Offer programs, not labels. Good programs are what students need."

Charlie finished his lunch and stood up to leave. "I've got to get back to work," he announced.

Sarah stood and hugged Charlie. "It was good seeing you again. Come by. Don't be a stranger."

"I won't be."

Charlie turned to Jane, winked at her, then left.

Jane sighed. "He sure did a good job of getting rid of the limiting messages he heard at school."

Sarah glanced at her, then looked away. "He was one of the lucky ones. Unfortunately, many don't question it. If the teacher says you can't, you can't."

Chapter 14

Is Special Education a Good Thing?

After lunch, Jane and Sarah wandered leisurely down the main street, stopping from time to time to look in the tourist shops. The stores sold everything from bathing suits, to T-shirts, to trays with pictures of palm trees and the words Key West printed across the top.

"I always thought that Special Education was a good thing. Students got the extra help they needed..." Jane looked questioningly at Sarah.

"All teachers should be trained to teach students as they need to learn. A teacher who is unable to help a student having difficulty is allowing that student to fall further and further behind. Unfortunately, when the students finally get the help they need, they are so far behind they have no hope of ever catching up."

Jane nodded knowingly.

"Students also learn from other students, sometimes more than they learn from their teachers, so sending them to special classes where all the students are having difficulty may actually compound their problems. Usually, there are no good role models."

"I never thought of it like that," Jane frowned.

"When I was teaching Special Education, I was asked to visit a student named Mary, who was attending school at a treatment center.

Her mother asked that she be placed in my class. Mary was considered to be developmentally challenged, or retarded. She also was too old to be in my primary class.

"At the treatment center, Mary was in a classroom with three other students, a teacher and a teacher's assistant. After observing her in the classroom, I attended a case conference on her. Everyone was present – psychologist, social worker, speech and language pathologist, etc. A file existed on Mary three inches thick! At the end of the meeting, I agreed to take Mary, even though I wasn't sure what her mother expected me to accomplish with her. The ratio in my class was twelve to one. Mary was nine, her language skills were minimal and the kids in my class were working several grade levels above her.

"Mary was in my class for only a short while when it became evident that she could do almost anything I asked of her, as long as she could understand what I wanted. I noticed she learned a great deal from watching the other children and imitating them. Her spelling and math skills soon surpassed those of the students in my class.

"I had Mary reassessed. It turned out she wasn't retarded, she was aphasic. She had difficulty understanding language, but had relatively normal intelligence. Mary went on to achieve academically; she learned a lot through singing and mimicking, and eventually won the school's public-speaking contest."

"I'm impressed."

Sarah looked away. "Unfortunately, she too got caught in the politics."

"What do you mean?"

"Mary was an unusual child. As she grew older, the school district didn't have an appropriate classroom placement for her, so she was often placed with students who had weird behaviors. Now remember, Mary learned from watching and mimicking others. Well, after a few years in these classrooms, Mary was assessed again."

"What were the test results?" Jane asked hesitantly.

"They said she was retarded."

"That's terrible! You must have felt awful."

"It broke my heart."

Jane was confused. "You don't believe in Special Education, yet you taught it?"

"I am not against students getting the help they need, I'm against what they have to go through in order to get that help. There are some special programs, I believe, we will always need. There are some children who may never be able to cope or learn in a regular classroom. But for the 'normal' children who aren't learning, they don't need labels and separate classrooms, they need good teaching. Every teacher should be trained to teach Special Education. Special Education is just good teaching. If regular classes were smaller and all teachers fully trained, students could be taught successfully, the way they need to be, right from the start."

Chapter 15

Learning to Share

Sarah and Jane settled down on Sarah's porch. Jane curled up on the swing. Sarah relaxed in her rocking chair.

"Sarah, how can I help my teachers become the best they can be?"

"First, how do you feel about yourself as an educator?"

"Me? I'm not too sure anymore," Jane answered.

"It's very hard to create in others what we don't feel in ourselves."

"That's true. I guess if I don't feel good about myself, it would be hard for me to instill those feelings in someone else."

"I have a few questions I'd like to ask you."

"Go ahead."

"When you were young, what labels were attached to you?"

"Me?" Jane looked confused.

"Were you the 'non-athletic one,' or the 'pretty one'? Did you have all the brains in the family? Were you the one who was going places, or the one nobody thought would ever amount to much?"

Jane thought for a moment. "I was the one who always had to try harder to be noticed. My younger sister, Susie, never did. She was the pretty one. People always used to talk about her looks... I wanted to be the pretty one."

"How did that make you feel?"

"I hated it. I felt like I would have to work hard to get ahead in this world and all Susie would have to do was look cute."

"In fact, you're very beautiful."

Jane smiled at Sarah's compliment.

"Have those feelings created a self-fulfilling prophecy in your life?"

"What do you mean?" Jane asked.

"Has being told that Susie was prettier than you and feeling that you would always have to work harder to get noticed in life, influenced the way you've done things? Has it affected the choices you've made in your life?"

Jane pondered Sarah's question. "I went out for everything in college – the debating club, the chess club. I wanted recognition, even if it was only for my brains. I guess I always felt like I was never good enough."

"Never good enough?"

"I know that sounds silly, but I always resented being compared to Susie. Actually, she's smart, too. She's a pharmacist. She has brains and looks."

"How do you think these feelings have affected the way you interact with other people?"

"I guess I've never allowed anyone to get too close to me…"

"Go on," Sarah urged.

"Because then they'd see the real me and know," Jane groped for the words, "how inadequate I really feel." She breathed out deeply. "I can't believe I said that! I've always tried to make sure everyone knows how intelligent I am. I have an opinion on everything."

Sarah asked, "Have the labels had an impact on you in terms of your career decisions?"

Jane reflected. "Yeah. I've always needed to stand out, to prove myself. I not only wanted to be a principal, but I had to be the youngest principal in the district. I made it, you know," Jane said proudly.

Sarah acknowledged her with a smile, and continued, "Now that you understand how your labels have been affecting you in the past, how do you think they'll affect you in the future?"

Jane paused for a moment. "I think… now I understand what's been driving me so hard to get the recognition I need. You know, I'm okay exactly the way I am."

"That's insightful. When we compare ourselves to others or allow the judgments of others to affect how we feel about ourselves, we're negating our own uniqueness, which is ours alone and very special. How did it feel to share?"

Jane laughed. "I never admitted to anyone before that I felt inadequate. I feel like I just let go of a big weight, a big secret."

Sarah grinned.

"It actually feels good to have said it," Jane sighed, her face relaxing.

"Self-acceptance can be a wonderful feeling."

Suddenly, Jane looked intently at Sarah, "But now that you know my secret, do you still like me?"

"You're still the same Jane. Sharing just helps me to understand your vulnerabilities and needs. It doesn't make you less lovable."

"It doesn't?"

"No. It allows me to love the real person, not the mask you present to the world. And when you know you're being loved for your true self, these feelings of acceptance will help you to feel truly proud of who you are."

Jane leaned over and hugged Sarah. "Thank you. I feel like that's the second time this week you've saved me… it sure feels good to hug someone. It's been awful not being allowed to hug the kids anymore."

"People need hugs. We all need hugs and feelings of being loved and accepted. Not allowing teachers to hug their students will be disastrous for the kids. Students will feel even more emotionally alone than they already do."

Jane hugged Sarah again. "It just feels good."

Chapter 16

Control versus Cooperation

Sarah, who had changed into shorts, T-shirt and a sun hat, brought out a tray of cold drinks. Jane eagerly took a glass of ginger ale from the tray and took a sip.

Sarah picked up her trowel, snippers and garden gloves and headed toward her vegetable garden.

"Can I help?" Jane asked, as she followed Sarah, glass in hand.

Sarah knelt in her garden and started pulling out the weeds. "Sure, grab the trowel."

Sarah handled her plants with loving tenderness. "I really enjoy taking care of my garden. It helps me to feel a special connection with the earth." She turned to Jane, who was busy digging up weeds. "Shall we continue our conversation?"

Jane smiled in appreciation. "Sarah, you've talked about teachers being models for harmonious behavior. But how do you let go of the control when that's all you've been used to?"

"We don't need to let go of anything. Rather, we replace it with something more constructive, more powerful. We need to understand that by controlling another person's behavior we are creating an atmosphere wherein students are only allowed to do what we want them to, when we want them to and how we want them to. It puts a great strain on them as well as on us. We need to learn to relate to students as human beings and not get caught up with the 'I'm the teacher' rules. Rules should only be used as guidelines. Teachers who need to control their students end up reducing their students' power and feelings of self-worth. But most important, they're teaching students to use control and manipulation in their relationships. Teachers who model love and caring teach students to relate harmoniously with one another. Then, there's no longer a need for control."

"It sounds nice, but how do you set this up in a classroom?"

"Start by inviting your students to have a great day with you. If you want your students to be wonderful – tell them they're wonderful, and keep telling them how much you appreciate their great behavior. Tell them how excited you are to be there with them and what interesting things you'll be doing together."

"Wouldn't they be cynical if a teacher said things like that?" Jane asked.

"Kids want to feel good and they want to have a great time. They'll give you the opportunity to live up to what you're saying and slowly you'll see you no longer need to control them. They're happy to cooperate with you because they feel good being a part of the program. If you need to control your students, the energy in the classroom is all yours and it quickly runs out. If your students are a part of creating the energy, wonderful things will happen. It's synergy."

"Synergy?"

"Synergy is everyone working together toward a common goal. It happens when the results of the group's efforts have a greater effect than that of an individual's."

"Sounds wonderful! It's like us working together in the garden." Jane grinned.

Sarah smiled, then stood up and brushed herself off. "Well, we're done here." She picked up her tools and headed over to the flower beds. Jane followed.

"There was one classroom I was invited into to work with the students, but before I had a chance to start, the teacher threatened the students with negative consequences if they misbehaved," Sarah grimaced. "After the threats, it didn't seem to matter what I did, I couldn't raise the energy level in the classroom. They all remained passive."

"I guess we spend too much time in school trying to control what's going on instead of letting the kids be a part of their own education."

Sarah laughed. "That's a great insight."

"Create goals and objectives using the curriculum, but let the curriculum evolve as part of the synergy," Jane concluded.

"I like that," Sarah grinned.

"Now, what am I going to do with all the rules at East County?"

"Give the students an opportunity to decide which ones they need and which ones they don't. In school, we're taught to obey rules without question. Teachers spend years training students to be compliant learners. But after graduation we expect them to be self-starters. Offer the students the opportunity to question the rules, to let their own needs and values surface."

"I guess most of us have been taught to play by the rules," Jane chuckled. "Now that I'm beginning to understand all my subconscious programming, I wish the real Jane would please stand up."

Sarah laughed as she snipped several roses from a bush. "I'm not surprised. After we've been raised by parents, taught by teachers, lived in a society or worked for a company, our own values get mixed up with the values of others, and sometimes the person inside of us gets lost in our desire to please those people. We try to get ahead in our careers by leadership cloning, by imitating the person ahead of us and losing ourselves in the process."

"I never thought of it like that."

"To find out who you really are, you need to separate the 'I shoulds' from the 'I want tos.' The 'I shoulds' are values and beliefs that are a part of you, but not yours. They're the parent or teacher in your head. They're the guilt words. By using the words 'I want to,' you may be surprised to discover the real Jane."

Jane thought about her life and career. What did she really want? Who was the real Jane?

She stood there quietly, in a quandary. Then suddenly she exclaimed, "I know who I am. Someone who has good intentions, but is only now discovering how to implement them."

Sarah laughed in support and gave her a rose.

Chapter 17

Limiting Learning

Sarah put the rest of the roses in a vase and placed them on the porch table. She looked at her watch, then toward the beach.

"Are you expecting someone?" Jane asked.

"My cousin Phil is vacationing not far from here. He said he would drop by this afternoon."

Jane got up from the swing. "I'll go then, I don't want to interfere with your visit."

"Please stay, I'd like you to meet him."

Jane was about to object when Phil rounded the corner of the house. He was in his late fifties, heavy set, with a full head of graying hair.

"Sarah!" he exclaimed.

Sarah rushed to give him a big hug. Then she turned and introduced him to Jane, adding, "She's a school principal."

Phil extended his hand. "Nice to meet you."

Jane liked Phil right away. He was well spoken and had the air of a successful professional.

After a few minutes of conversation, Sarah said, "Phil, tell Jane how a principal changed your life."

Phil seemed to be reticent. "I don't like to tell that story. I... I feel... funny about it."

"Please Phil," Jane urged. "I'm always interested in how

principals have influenced their students."

Phil looked at Jane's eager face, then relented and sat down next to her on the swing. "When I was in ninth grade, the principal called me into his office. I remember I used to be very scared of the man. Well, as I stood there shaking in front of him, he told me I was wasting my time in school. He said I should quit and get a job."

Shocked, Jane asked, "Why?"

"You see, I was in a class called the Opportunity Class. I didn't realize it at the time, but what they really meant was 'no opportunity.' It was a class for students who were experiencing difficulty learning. But it really didn't matter why he told me to quit. In those days, you didn't argue with the principal. So I quit school and went to work."

"What did you do?"

"I went to work up in the Arctic on the DEW line."

"DEW line?"

"It stands for Distant Early Warning. It's a chain of radar stations."

"Oh," Jane nodded.

"My foreman on the DEW line was a good guy. He saw some potential in me and suggested I finish high school."

"Did you?"

"Yeah, I did. I finished high school at night."

"That's great," Jane smiled.

Sarah interrupted. "Tell her what you did next."

"I went to college."

"Remarkable. Did you finish?"

Phil nodded.

Sarah's face lit up as she said, "Only after he got a Ph.D. in Engineering."

Jane's jaw dropped. "A Ph.D. in Engineering?" She stared at Phil, to make sure she'd heard right.

Phil grinned in acknowledgment.

"Then he taught at the Massachusetts Institute of Technology and worked on the United States space program."

"Why were you asked to quit school?"

"I really don't know. Maybe it was because I was disorganized," Phil shrugged.

Sarah added, "Our judgments about our students' abilities aren't always right. We can't see into their souls. We're only privileged to see a small part of their potential. Yet we judge them and act toward them as if we're all-knowing. We are often wrong."

"But this happened a long time ago. Surely we as educators are no longer counseling students to quit school," Jane insisted.

"Not long ago, when I was a Special Education consultant, a student of mine, Diane, who was in a special class for slow learners, was re-tested and found to be working at grade level for her age. She had been in a special class since third grade. Now, because of the new test results, she was being placed in a regular seventh grade classroom."

Jane was impressed. "That's wonderful. I know that doesn't happen very often. Usually students placed in Special Education classes don't seem to be able to ever catch up enough to get back into a regular classroom."

"Then you can understand why Diane was so proud of herself. She had achieved something very rare. Diane talked excitedly about going on to a regular junior high. She wanted to be a doctor."

"Did she make it?" Jane asked.

"In a promotion meeting with Diane's seventh grade teacher and the school principal, I learned they were planning on having Diane repeat seventh grade."

"Couldn't she do the work?"

"Up until then I had been told that the placement was going

well. So I asked Diane's teacher how she was doing, compared to the rest of the class.

"Her teacher said that her work was about average with the middle group. I asked if any of the other students from that group were being repeated. She shook her head. Just as I was about to look at the principal for support, he voiced concern about Diane's desire to become a doctor. He felt he should counsel her to look for a different profession, maybe a nurse's aide.

"Needless to say, I was astounded. Whether Diane's desire to become a doctor was reasonable or not was not the question. It was whether or not the teacher and the principal had a right to discourage this young lady who had improved so much."

"Where did Diane end up?" Jane asked.

"Unfortunately, I was unable to convince the principal and teacher to promote Diane. But some kids, no matter how hard we try to discourage them, won't give up. Diane finished high school and is now attending college."

"That's quite a story." Jane stared at Sarah.

"I'm glad to hear Diane's making her own decisions," Phil added. "I'd hate for her to think she wasn't capable just because her teacher or principal told her so."

Jane looked from Phil to Sarah.

"Diane was unusual," Sarah continued, "to most students, how a teacher judges them is very important. The labels put on them often limit their chances in life. Think of all those report cards and all the heartaches we've caused students who were told they weren't smart enough, or capable enough. What a teacher says and does has a lasting effect. But we leave out the most important opinion of all, teaching our students to trust their own judgments about themselves, to believe in themselves."

"I guess the more we've been trying to change things, the more they've stayed the same," Jane frowned.

Sarah agreed. "Because we haven't tried to change the right things. We should be teaching students to be proud of who they are, to honor and respect their special talents and abilities, not discourage them and take away their dreams. Each day in school, students are being compared to their classmates. The reality is that none of us can ever measure up to anyone else. Imagine if Phil and I had to compete against each other. We don't have the same abilities. I could never be an engineer like Phil; I don't have the same talents he does. Compared to him, I'd look like a failure."

"And I don't have Sarah's patience and insights for working with students," Phil added.

Sarah smiled. "But as long as students are continually being compared, they'll have little self-esteem left by the time they're out of kindergarten."

Jane thought of Bobby Mendez. He was so talented as an artist, yet all he ever heard in school was how poorly he was reading and writing compared to the other students in his class. Very few students could draw like Bobby, yet his teacher wasn't celebrating his special talent or making him feel unique. If anything, he felt like a failure.

Chapter 18

Evaluation for Validation

Phil stood up to leave. Sarah got up and hugged him. "I'm glad you came by."

"So am I," Phil said as he waved good-by to Jane, and left.

"Sarah if we don't compare students, how do we grade them?"

"Instead of grading students, we need to show them how to improve. We need to show them how to become better at what they're doing without the penalty of low marks or humiliation for trying. Students need to be a part of their own evaluation process."

"You mean teach kids how to evaluate themselves?"

"Learning to evaluate how we're doing in life is a very important skill. Once we're out of school, how else will we know how we're doing if we don't know how to evaluate our own progress?"

Jane nodded. "I guess you're right."

"Students can help us understand what motivates them, how they learn best, what their interests and goals are. It can be a phenomenal experience for both the teacher and student."

Jane raised her eyebrows as she thought of the possibilities.

"I once knew a student named Josh who was in the first grade," Sarah continued. "He was wonderfully bright and articulate but wasn't making much academic progress. His teacher tried every method she could think of to help him learn, but didn't have much success. It was only when she gave him the responsibility for his own progress that she started to see an improvement in his work. With his teacher's help, he learned to set his own goals in relation to the first grade program. He then charted his own progress. By becoming an active participant in his own learning, his work started to improve."

"But what about grades? Colleges demand grades."

"As schools start to change the way they evaluate students, colleges may begin to realize the value of having students who can set goals and chart their own progress. These are valuable skills. Think of all the college students who don't make it because they can't handle being responsible for their own learning."

"This all sounds nice, but rather utopian," Jane interjected.

"I didn't say changing the world would be easy," Sarah laughed.

"That you didn't," Jane agreed.

"When teachers set academic goals with students, to decide what they'll learn and how they'll learn it, they're empowering their students. Many teachers don't realize that by giving more responsibility to students, they're enabling their passive students to become active learners, in control of their own lives and futures."

"I like that."

"It's the same with evaluations. Students, who are being compared or evaluated by teachers, are giving over their personal power to someone else, and that's a powerless position. How many kids see themselves as victims? People that life happens *to*? Who don't use their power, or make good choices in life?"

"Many," Jane agreed.

"Students who are given the responsibility for evaluating their own progress are being given a chance to take charge of their own destiny and become empowered decision-makers."

"Teenagers have always said they want more control over their lives," Jane added. "I guess we haven't been listening to them. We just keep on doing the same old things, thinking it will eventually sink in. Maybe that's why we lose so many students to drugs and gangs."

Sarah nodded. "Not only is our thinking habitual, it's not working. By teaching students to set personal and academic goals, by giving them power over their failures and successes, we can show them their destiny becomes not something that *happens* to them, but something they *create*. Do you know what this type of understanding is important for?"

Jane looked at Sarah for the answer.

"Developing self-esteem. And once students understand this, they'll no longer look outside themselves for validation, nor will they base how they feel about themselves on what other people say, or on how other people act toward them."

"That really is empowering."

"Self-confidence and feelings of self-worth are the most important qualities we can instill in our students. People who have good self-esteem are willing to take responsible risks and become leaders in our society, and we need good leaders."

"Sarah, do you really think you can change the world?"

"I learned long ago I can't change the world; I can only change how I relate to the world. My mission in life has been to help my students feel connected, capable, empowered and loved, helping them to create better lives for themselves. And when life becomes better for kids, the future becomes better for us all."

"Then I guess if I want to change what's happening in my school, I have to change myself first."

"I once heard this Hindu proverb," Sarah added. "'There is nothing noble about being superior to someone else. The true nobility is in being superior to your previous self.'"

Chapter 19

Reaching for a Dream

Sarah and Jane heard the sound of a jet-ski. They turned toward the water's edge as James pulled up onto the beach.

James ran up to them. "Sarah! Jane! Guess what?"

He took a second to catch his breath. "I'm going back to school. I'm going to be a teacher!"

"That's wonderful!" Sarah enthused. "You'll be great with the kids."

James plunked himself down on the porch swing. "It's always been my dream. I've decided to make it come true."

Jane beamed. "That's great."

"I've always known that teaching was a calling," James said excitedly. "It's the most important job in the universe. Teachers have the future of the world in their hands."

Sarah smiled. "Yes, teachers have the power to make a difference in this world. We can empower kids, or put them down. We can help them become responsible citizens, or needy individuals."

"Sarah," Jane said hesitantly, "I overheard some of my teachers complaining in the teachers' lounge. It really worries me because even my good teachers are starting to sound disillusioned and unhappy. I don't know how to stop it. Sometimes... I find it even affects me. I try to be up and positive, but it becomes almost impossible in that atmosphere."

"Negativity is contagious, even toxic. Unfortunately, if that kind of negativity is going on and it's accepted behavior, the new teachers, the ones you've hired because of their high energy and enthusiasm, will start to talk and act that way to fit in."

"Really?" Jane was dismayed.

Sarah nodded. "New teachers don't want to look like eager beavers if everyone else is a complainer. They'd get ostracized, so they lower their standards to fit in. These norms in a school are very powerful."

"I guess it's up to me to raise the standards," Jane said.

"It's not easy, once they've been set," Sarah sympathized.

"I've been trying to make the teachers at my school change, but somehow..." Jane shook her head.

"You cannot *make* someone change," James stated. "Change can only come from within, and no one can make you look inside if you don't want to. Believe me. I know."

"I guess that's true," Jane frowned.

Sarah added, "Teachers who come to a place within themselves where they're happy and proud of who they are, have internal feelings of self-worth and self-esteem. Then their ability to pass on these good feelings to their students multiplies a hundredfold. But if your teachers don't feel good about themselves, it's difficult for them to help their students feel good."

"What does this have to do with changing the norms in my school?"

"Teachers who aren't afraid to be themselves are able to reject behaviors that aren't theirs. They set their own norms."

"Then it's up to me to create the desire for change in my teachers," Jane stated firmly.

Sarah smiled. "Once your teachers learn to look inward and unmask their true selves, they'll never again be able to act negatively as they did before. When teachers are in touch with their own integrity and acting from their heart consciousness, not only you and I, but every teacher will be a part of changing the world for the better."

"Right on!" James grinned.

The sun was starting its descent. Jane and Sarah stood on the white sandy beach waving good-by to James as his jet-ski disappeared into the horizon. Then they strolled down the beach, stopping occasionally to watch the sea gulls dive, and marvel at their accuracy. Each dive produced a fish.

Jane spoke up. "Why are parents always asking us to go back to the good old days, if things weren't so great back then?"

"Don't forget, the majority of us were taught in that same habitual system. Most people don't know of any other, let alone better, way of teaching children. They feel that if it was good enough for them, it's good enough for their kids. What they don't understand is what was done to them. How they were programmed to think negatively about themselves. How their inner power was limited, or taken away from them. The author Robertson Davies said it very well: 'The world is full of people whose notion of a satisfactory future is, in fact, a return to an idealized past.' If we keep idealizing the past and head into the future looking backward, we'll fall butt first into our graves, never having had the guts to enjoy the opportunities that await us."

"We always seem to remember the past as being better than it was," Jane frowned. "Many people are afraid of change, but change can mean growth, a chance for inner transformation."

"You're an excellent student," Sarah remarked.

"That's because you're such a great teacher!"

Sarah grinned. "I knew there was a point to this conversation when we started it a few days ago."

"I guess I should sign your plaque, 'To a Great Teacher from a devoted Principal.'"

"You know, I kind of like that. It has a nice ring to it."

They both laughed, and continued their stroll down the beach.

Chapter 20

The Mission

Jane stood at the shoreline, gazing out at the clear, blue ocean. The cool, morning tide washed up onto the shore and slapped against her feet, then quickly retreated. Jane inhaled the refreshing ocean air. She felt wonderful.

"I wish I could stay here forever," she sighed.

She reflected on how much she had learned in such a short period of time. It was now clear to her why she and Sarah had crossed paths. She hadn't been able to make any changes back at East County because she hadn't known what changes were needed. All she really was doing was acting habitually, playing a familiar tune. Her teachers knew that tune and also knew that if they waited long enough, that song would pass and then there would be a new one to be ignored. They had learned long ago that if they held out long enough, there would be no need to change.

Jane now understood why there was such an urgent need for change in her school, and in every school. She also knew it was her job to help her teachers shift from teaching curriculum to teaching people. She thought back to the toxic conversations she'd heard in the teachers' lounge, how trashing kids and the system was sanctioned behavior in her school, and the norm in many schools. Even her new teachers were modeling the negative behaviors and lowering themselves to the standards of the worn-out, indifferent teachers. By allowing those norms to be the standard in her school, she had set her teachers and students up for failure. Teachers needed to be in their classrooms because they loved to work with kids, not because they were waiting for their pensions.

Helping students create a better life for themselves had been Sarah's desire when she had gone into teaching. Jane, too, wanted to make a difference. She wanted to create schools that offered students the feelings of safety and caring they needed to be able to risk discovering their limitless potential.

Chapter 21

Sailing

Jane sat in Sarah's rocking chair, enjoying the peaceful sound of the ocean waves. A sailboat was heading their way.

Sarah stood as she watched the sailor pull his boat onto the beach.

"Hi Charlie!" Sarah waved as soon as he jumped out of his boat.

Charlie hurried up to the house. "Hi Sarah, Jane."

"Good to see you." Sarah welcomed him.

"I thought Jane might like to go for a sail before she heads home tomorrow," Charlie said to Sarah, then looked at Jane. "Would you like to try some Florida fun?"

Jane felt her eyes light up. "I'd love it."

"I promise not to run out of gas," he laughed.

Jane got up from the comfortable rocker and looked longingly at it for a moment. She promised herself she would get one and it would be just like Sarah's. Then sadly she looked at Sarah. She went to her, arms open, and gave her a big warm hug. "I can never thank you enough."

"The gifts you will bring to your students is my thanks. Now, go for it, go for it all!" Sarah whispered in her ear.

Jane turned and smiled happily at Charlie. He reached for her hand, as they ran toward the sailboat.

Part Two

The Awakening

Chapter 22

Returning to School

"Teen Violence Tied to Feelings of Isolation." Jane read the headline in her morning newspaper. Loneliness was leading young people to violence, crime and even suicide, the article said.

As Jane sipped her morning coffee at the small round oak table in her condominium kitchen, she thought back to her talks with Sarah. Sarah had emphasized how important it was for students to feel cared for, to feel accepted by their teachers and peers. She had stressed how important it was for teachers to give students this sense of belonging in the classroom because, for some students, it might be the only place they'd receive it.

Today was Jane's first day back at school since the Spring Break. In Florida, talking about all the improvements she was going to make seemed so easy. But now, back in Pittsburgh, could she really create the changes in her teachers and school that she now knew were so crucial for the mental health of her students, and for the future of society? It was such a big job. *You have to have the dream before you can make it a reality*, she thought.

Jane got up from the table, checked her watch, picked up her briefcase and headed toward the door.

Arriving home last night after being in the warmth and sunshine for a week was difficult. The city looked dark and bleak. It was like the challenge in front of her, to change the bleakness in her school to sunshine and warmth.

As Jane entered the school office, she was greeted by her secretary, Sandy, a kind, middle-aged woman, who had been at East County Elementary School since it opened twenty-two years ago.

"Bill Carson called." Sandy handed Jane a pink message slip.

"Thanks." Jane looked around the reception office and greeted a few of her teachers, who were preparing for their first day back, then headed into her office.

She put her briefcase down and sat back in her chair. If she were going to set a new example and make changes, she had to start now. She got up from her chair and headed out.

As Jane entered the teachers' lounge, she spotted Peter Hopkins and Lillian Campbell having coffee together. Jane went toward them, a smile on her face. "Glorious day, isn't it?"

"You must be kidding! It's cold, and it's supposed to rain. I hate this weather," Lillian frowned.

"The break was just too short for me," Peter added. "I don't know if I can face those kids today." He shook his head.

Jane hesitated, unsure what to say. The toxic environment was already permeating her school and the first class of the day hadn't begun yet. She had to do something. "What would you need to make this a better day?" Jane asked.

Peter and Lillian looked at each other, as if they weren't sure.

"What can I do to help turn this negative day into one that will help you feel excited to be here?" Jane probed.

Fran Lopez, overhearing the conversation, answered, "I want to be able to enjoy my students. I became a teacher because I love working with kids, but I have so many behavior problems in my class I don't have the time to have any fun with them."

Barbara Jones, also listening, added, "I find the kids so hard to control. They never listen anymore."

"Yeah." Carole Chan joined the chorus, as if it were becoming a free-for-all grumbling session. "The kids don't pay attention to the rules. Even though they're in Special Education, they should be able to follow a few simple rules."

Jane took a deep breath; she could feel herself getting riled. Anger would not solve anything. She pushed away her negative feelings, and asked, "If we could figure out a way for teaching to become enjoyable and exciting, how many of you would want to participate in that discovery process?"

Fran answered, "I would love it."

"Would we figure out new ways to control the kids?" asked Barb.

"How about the rules? I think we need more rules and tougher penalties," Carole added.

Lillian, who had been sitting on the sidelines, nodded vigorously. "I agree with that. No more talking. I can't stand all their talking."

Peter approved. "And let's not promote kids until they're ready and can do the work. It's too hard on the next teacher. My class is full of kids who should never have passed first grade."

Jane was starting to feel discouraged. What would Sarah say to them? Jane calmed herself and thought for a moment, then answered, "We'll explore all the possibilities and come up with great solutions. You're a great team to work with and I want you all to be here giving the students your best. The future of our world depends on us."

"The future of our world? How do you figure that?" Peter asked skeptically.

"When you're retired and living on your pension, what generation of individuals do you think will be in power, controlling that pension?"

"I never thought of it that way," he said mindfully.

"We're raising the next generation of leaders, business people, doctors, teachers. We have the power to mold our future society. We can give it our best and educate our students to be responsible, independent, capable individuals, or we can demean and control them into becoming passive, unhappy, irresponsible people. We have that choice. We have that power. They're ours to influence. We have the most important profession in the universe. How many of you are with me to help create the greatest school in this country?"

"Sure," Fran nodded and looked uncertainly at the others.

"Yeah," Carole said without conviction.

"We'll see," Barb muttered as she left the room.

"Well, maybe." Peter was not persuaded.

"I don't know." Lillian shook her head skeptically.

Jane's gaze shifted from one teacher to the next as they spoke.

Chapter 23

Journey of Discovery

Jane finally reached Bill after playing telephone tag with him all day.

"How was your holiday?" he asked.

"It was wonderful. I can't wait to tell you all about it."

"Did you give up your notion about wanting to change the world?"

"No. I've decided to take up the challenge."

"Don't waste your time. We live in a tough, unforgiving world."

"Is that what I should be teaching my students?"

"Jane, I just want you to be realistic."

"How about rather than accepting the world the way it is, I do my best to try and improve it. Especially since, as an educational administrator, I'm in a position to make a difference."

"That rest did you good. I hear Jane 'the fighter' in your voice."

"I never was a quitter."

"Let me know how you make out."

"I'll be in touch." Jane hung up the phone and sighed as she thought about the big challenge ahead of her.

Jane called a special staff meeting for that afternoon.

Her agenda was simple: rekindle the love of teaching in her teachers. She knew that without winning over her staff, nothing would improve for the students.

The teachers gathered in the library. Jane watched as they sat in two's and three's with their friends around the rectangular table. They chatted amicably among themselves. Jane thought, *these are the same teachers that want to deny their students any kind of socializing in the classroom, impose strict codes of behavior and have no-talking rules.* Jane remembered her insight with Sarah while walking on the beach: "Treat your students as you yourself would like to be treated." Would she be able to help her teachers come to this important realization, just as Sarah had helped her?

Jane called the meeting to order. "I want to thank you all for your willingness to participate in this discovery process. Before we get down to business, I thought it might be helpful if we each knew a little more about the wonderful people we're working with."

The teachers looked at each other, as if pleased they were so well thought of by their principal.

"I want each of you to write on a piece of paper ten of your teaching accomplishments that you're most proud of. They can be personal achievements, or because of your guidance and assistance, the accomplishments of some of your students. The list may contain anything that has happened to you that you consider to be your personal success in the field of education."

The teachers looked confused.

Jane clarified, "An accomplishment could be getting your degree, helping Johnny overcome a learning block, helping students solve problems in their lives..."

"Will we have to share these?" Peter asked.

"Only if you feel comfortable," Jane answered.

Some of the teachers started their list. Others looked around as if waiting for further instructions but, seeing their colleagues writing, they too began to write.

Jane worked on her own list, thinking back to her achievements and her need to be noticed. She had won several chess trophies at college and had almost finished first in her class when she took flying lessons. The flying lessons had been a challenge. She had wanted to overcome her fear of flying. She did!

Jane thought proudly of the time she had coached the girls' high school basketball team and they had won the city championship. And then, of course, there was Cria, darling little Cria. She would do anything to please the boys. Jane had helped her to become a top basketball player. Cria's growing self-confidence meant she no longer said 'yes' to the boys who only wanted sexual favors. Jane also remembered Paula, a ward of the state, whom she had befriended and helped to get placed in an adoptive home.

Jane looked around. Some of her teachers were still writing, others were thinking. Jane continued with her list. She thought of some of her other students, the ones who still came to visit her, even though it had been years since she had taught them. There was Salvadore, who had been so lost when he first arrived in her class from Mexico. He lived with his grandparents and hardly spoke any English. She had worked with him every day after school, tutoring him and helping him to integrate himself into the school and the community. In his last year of high school, he had been the school valedictorian – his English was perfect!

As Jane continued reminiscing, she felt her pride growing in herself and in her profession. Her job was indeed to help make life better for kids. How could she have forgotten how much she loved working with her students and helping them learn and grow?

The room was quiet and Jane wondered if her teachers were feeling as exhilarated by the exercise as she was.

She added to her list Christine, the abused runaway. Jane had been instrumental in getting help for both Christine and her family.

Then there was Matthew. She had helped him to realize that losing his leg did not mean he no longer had value as a human being. Jane added becoming a principal to her list of achievements, feeling a special pride at having been given the opportunity to make a difference in students' lives. And of course there was Sarah. Spending a week with Sarah had renewed her faith in herself as an educator and as an advocate of change. Sarah had inspired her to try and reach new heights in her career.

Jane put down her pencil and looked up. Most of the teachers were finished. The atmosphere was calm and pensive.

Jane began, "How are you feeling after that exercise?"

A few hands went up.

"A little surprised and proud," Barb answered.

"Reflective," added Fran.

"Does anyone feel comfortable sharing their list?"

A few teachers nodded.

"Great, but before we begin, there are three things I'd like us to consider, to allow those who wish to share an additional level of comfort. Before asking the sharer a question, please relate something about yourself first."

Jane looked in Peter's direction as he raised his hand. "Yes?"

"I don't understand what you mean."

"If there's something on my list you want me to clarify, I'd appreciate it if you would first share something from your own experience that relates to the question. That way, I won't feel intimidated by the question, and will understand where the question is coming from."

"Oh, okay."

"The next suggestion is that we don't give the sharers any advice, or tell them what they should have done. We want people to feel safe in relating their experiences and not feel judged."

Several heads nodded.

"The last consideration and probably the most important is that whatever is shared in this room is confidential and that the confidentiality is not just for an hour or for today, but forever. I would like us to agree that whatever people say here is not to be discussed or shared outside of this room, unless you're discussing it with the person who shared. Is there anyone who has any problems with my suggestions?"

"Why do we need confidentiality?" Fran asked.

"When people are asked to share their experiences, they're usually more comfortable if they know that whatever they say will not come back later to haunt them."

"Good point," Fran agreed.

"Any other questions?" Jane looked around the room. "Who would like to go first?"

Lillian called out, "Why don't you go first?" Her voice had a slight edge to it.

Jane acknowledged her with a smile. "Good idea." She began to read her list.

When Jane finished, Barb put up her hand. "I'd like to go next."

"Great."

As the teachers each found the confidence to share their successes, wonderful stories filled the room. Stories about how they had helped students overcome difficulties in school, in their homes and in their personal lives. Each and every teacher remembered times of adversity with their students and how they had overcome these problems with wonderful results. Jane felt proud. She realized she was working with a truly dedicated group of teachers.

As each teacher had a turn, the energy in the room rose. When the exercise was finished, Jane waited as the teachers conversed among themselves, sharing their experiences with each other on a more personal level.

Chapter 24

Feeling Safe

As the talking started to die down, Jane asked, "How did it feel to share?"

"I felt really safe sharing here," Jody responded. "I'm not sure why."

"Yeah, I did too. I think it was because I knew that I wasn't going to be judged," Barb volunteered.

"I liked the confidentiality," Peter stated. "It allowed me to speak the truth without worrying about what might happen later."

"I liked the fact that we've had so many similar experiences. It was amazing to find out we've all gone through a lot of the same things," Carole responded. "I learned such interesting things about the people I work with. We really are a great group."

Jane smiled. "Yes, you are. Now, I would like each of you to pair up with another member of the staff, someone you don't know well."

She waited as the teachers moved about the room looking for partners.

"For this exercise, I have two additional suggestions I would like you to try and incorporate in your sharing. I would like the person who's doing the talking to be specific about the information they're sharing, and also to use 'I' statements. In other words, speak from your own experience."

"You mean we shouldn't say, 'You know how it is when you

don't follow the rules,' " Barb mocked the rule.

The staff laughed.

"You got it," said Jane.

"Shouldn't you say, 'I' got it?" Lillian smirked.

"Okay, I see that you understand. What I want you to do now is to share with your partner, who was your favorite teacher, and why? Each of you take three minutes. Begin now."

The din in the room rose as the teachers shared their stories with each other. Jane watched how animated and excited they became as they described their favorite teachers.

At the end of the exercise, Jane asked, "Is there anyone willing to share their story with the whole group?"

All the hands went up.

Stories were told about how each of them was made to feel special by a caring teacher. How being with that teacher helped them to feel successful and motivated to do well academically. It was usually this teacher who had inspired them to go into the teaching profession.

"Let's list the qualities in these teachers that were most important for you when you went to school." Jane used a marker and chart paper to write the list. The teachers called out the words: caring, motivating, non-judgmental, good listeners, were able to explain their subject clearly, fair, inspiring, helpful, tolerant, funny, charitable, conscientious, intuitive, non-demeaning, understanding, knew when to back off, did not embarrass, not rigid.

Jane was excited by the list. "If these qualities were important to you when you went to school, do you think they're important to your students?"

The room fell silent.

"In the teachers' lounge this morning, many of you wanted to find better ways of controlling your students. You wanted more rules and tougher penalties. Yet I don't see those things on this list. Could it be that when teachers displayed these characteristics," Jane pointed to the list, "and instead, created a rapport with their students, that there was less of a need for tougher penalties and more discipline?"

"But kids have changed. They're not like they used to be," Peter protested.

"Peter, when you first started teaching, did you teach the same way you do now?" Jane asked.

"Of course not."

"What's the difference?"

Peter looked down as he thought about it. "Me," he answered. "I'm not the same. I don't have the same patience I used to have."

"If I had started this meeting intolerant of all of your talking and moved each of you away from the people you feel safest with, what do you think would have happened in this meeting?"

Fran put up her hand. "I, for one, would've shut down."

"I would've listened, but I wouldn't have said anything," Barb volunteered.

"But you gave us rules for sharing," Lillian protested.

"You're right, I did give you suggestions to help the group with the sharing process. What did the rules do?"

"They made me feel safer," Jody answered. "At first I thought they were just more rules to conform to, but then I realized they were just suggestions to help me be myself. As suggestions, they didn't feel as intimidating."

Margaret added, "I agree. The suggestions allowed me to communicate better. I'm going to try them in my class. I want to see if I can improve the way my students listen to each other."

"I've always struggled trying to conform to everyone else's rules," said Carole.

"Then why are we doing it to our students?" Jane asked.

"Do unto others…," Fran's voice trailed off.

The teachers looked at one another in amazement.

Barb finished the statement, "As you would have them do unto you."

"It's that simple, isn't it?" Fran said.

Jane nodded. "Yes."

Chapter 25

Maintaining Classroom Control

The next morning, when Jane entered the teachers' lounge, she tried to gauge the mood of her teachers. The sounds of the conversations were softer and more personal. There was no grumbling.

Carole Chan approached Jane. She was carrying several heavy books. Jane noted the title on top, *Maintaining Classroom Control.* "I thought a lot about our meeting last night," Carole sighed. "I wish I didn't have to spend all day enforcing rules, but I really don't know what else to do. If I don't, my students go wild."

"How do your students feel about the rules?"

"They don't say much. They just do as they please. They have no respect for the rules."

"Then the rules aren't doing any good, are they?"

"No, they're not working."

"What if you sat down with your students and asked them which rules they think are necessary and why they think they need those rules."

"I could do that, but what then?"

"Ask them if they'll participate with you in observing those rules."

"Why should they want to obey any rules?" asked Carole.

"Because they'll have given you the reasons they need those particular rules. Offer to get rid of all the others – the ones they feel they don't need."

"What if they get rid of the important ones?"

"You mean the ones they aren't listening to anyway? At least this way you'll gain some of their cooperation and enlist their help in setting the tone of the classroom. Are the rules meant to meet your needs or your students'?"

"They don't meet anyone's now. But I'm the teacher, I know what the students need," Carole protested.

Jane thought about what Sarah had said about rules, how teachers who needed to control their students reduced their students' power and feelings of self-worth. "I'm sure you do," Jane agreed. "But students also need to feel empowered, to feel they have control over their lives. Don't get caught up with the 'I'm-the-teacher' rules. Rules are only meant to be guidelines. Spending your day trying to control your students takes a lot of your energy."

"I'll say," Carole agreed.

"If you invite your students to participate in creating a great day with you, then the energy expended isn't all yours, it's shared with your students. Your students will feel more empowered and you'll no longer need to control them through rules. You'll have their cooperation."

Carole looked skeptical and almost relieved as she heard the morning bell ring. "I'll try," was all she said as she scurried off to her classroom.

Chapter 26

The Problem Student

Jane checked her morning mail. There was a postcard from Charlie, wishing her luck making the changes at East County. *How nice of him to offer his support!* She smiled as she slipped the card into her pocket.

Jane thought back to their last afternoon together, sailing. The day had been glorious, the sky cloudless. The winds carried the boat through the waves at a quick clip. Charlie handled the boat masterfully.

After the sail, they had dinner together. Charlie told her he rarely left his store during the day, but the afternoon he rescued her, business had been slow. He had decided to take his motorboat out for a ride, and luckily, came upon her and her disabled jet-ski. He felt it was fate.

Jane didn't really understand a lot about fate. But she did know, that not only had Charlie saved her life, but he had been an important catalyst for providing her with one of the most enlightening experiences of her life – meeting Sarah.

Jane looked down at her desk and picked up the East County Elementary School Student Handbook. She leafed through it. The first three pages were full of rules of behavior. As she skimmed through the rules, she noted most of them demanded rigid conformity; there wasn't much room for students to be themselves.

Jane frowned. She definitely needed to make some changes here. She decided she would set up a committee of students from all the grades to review the rules and offer their input.

Sandy entered Jane's office. "Barb has sent Gordon to see you."

"Did she say why?"

"The usual – disrupting the class."

"Send him in."

Try to understand the students' problems from their point of view, Jane recalled Sarah saying. She hoped it would work with Gordon.

Gordon entered, a look of defiance on his face. He was ready to do battle.

Jane got up from behind her desk and went to sit at the round table in her office. She invited Gordon to join her. He looked suspiciously at her, but complied.

"What happened?" Jane said gently.

"It wasn't my fault," Gordon protested.

"Tell me what went on."

"I had to hit Sonia," Gordon said matter-of-factly.

Jane nodded, she could feel her anger rising. She pushed it away and continued gently, "Why? What did she do?"

"She moved my paper. She made me make a mistake. I don't like to make mistakes."

"We can learn a lot from making mistakes. Mistakes aren't necessarily all bad."

Gordon looked at her as if to say, who are you kidding? "Sonia pushed my hand and she made me make this big line on my paper. She ruined my work."

"Did she do it on purpose?"

"I don't know."

"Do you have an eraser?"

"Yeah, but I shouldn't have to erase something she did!"

"Hitting or hurting anyone in this school is not allowed. We have to learn to tell people how we feel and ask them to please be careful when they're around us, so they don't push our hands."

"My dad said the only way to get their attention is to punch them in the mouth."

"Where's your dad now?"

Gordon shrugged. "My mom won't let me see him."

"Has he tried to come back home?"

"He wanted to see me but my mom won't let him."

"Did she tell you why?"

"Because he hurts people. She doesn't want him to hurt me or her anymore."

"Did he hit your mom?"

"Only when she needed it."

Jane tried to hide her revulsion. She continued softly, "Your mom cares a lot about you, doesn't she?"

Gordon shrugged again. "I don't know."

"Do you believe her, when she says she doesn't want you to be hurt by your dad?"

"My dad's a great guy. He just likes to beat people up. I want to be just like him."

Jane felt discouraged; the conversation was going in circles. "Gordon, laws are made to protect people. It's against the law to physically hurt another person. You're such a great young man; it's sad that you hurt someone. No one likes to be hurt. I'm sure you didn't like it when your dad hurt you?"

Gordon looked away. "He said he did it 'cause he had to." He turned back and stared at Jane. "You know what? He didn't really have to."

"Why not?" Jane asked.

"He should have just told me. I'm not a dummy."

"Do you understand why you didn't have to hit Sonia?"

"She's not a dummy either?"

"No, she isn't. I think she probably pushed your arm by accident. What do you think?"

Gordon nodded. "Probably."

"What do you think you should do when you go back to your classroom?"

"Say I'm sorry."

Jane nodded, "Sounds good to me. Now go back to your class."

Gordon looked surprised. "You're not going to suspend me?"

Jane thought for a moment. "Do I need to?"

Gordon shook his head. "No."

"Then get back to your class."

Gordon bounced out of Jane's office.

Chapter 27

The Vengeful Teacher

Moments later, Barb stormed into Jane's office. "Why did you send Gordon back to class?"

"Didn't he apologize to Sonia?"

"An apology is not enough."

"What's the problem now?"

"He's a troublemaker. I don't want him in my class."

"Does he know that?"

"You better believe he does. That kid's going to be a delinquent. You'll see. I'm never wrong about those kids."

Jane grimaced. "You'll get what you expect."

"Huh?"

"Whatever you expect his behavior to be, is what you'll get."

"Well, I don't exactly tell him to misbehave. He does that well enough on his own."

"You've labeled him a delinquent and your voice, your body language and all your interactions with him are carrying that message. Students try to live up to their teacher's expectations." Jane struggled to hide her annoyance.

"Hey, wait a minute! I didn't start this. He had problems with his last year's teacher, too."

"Barbara, each school year offers the student a new opportunity, a fresh start. Your talents as a teacher may have been just what Gordon needed to do better at school. Did you ever give him a chance? Did you ever expect great things from him?"

Barb thought for a moment. "You know he comes from such a bad home."

"Does that mean there's no place on this earth where he can feel safe and cared for? Nowhere he can learn to create a positive future for himself? A future not modeled after his home life, but after the caring teachers he was lucky enough to have at school?"

Barb's eyes narrowed as she protested, "Jane, I've tried, but you don't know him like I do."

"I may not, but I do know his emotional needs are not being met at home nor at school. Gordon can't ask you for the caring he needs, because he doesn't even know that's what he needs."

Barb looked dubiously at Jane, who continued gently, "Try talking to him as if he's already behaving the way you want him to. If you want him to be great, tell him he's great. If you want him to do good work, tell him he's doing good work. You might get a big surprise. He may live up to your new expectations."

Barb shifted her weight uncomfortably as Jane said, "We can be wrong about students' abilities and where they'll end up in life. I met a man last week who was told he was going nowhere and to quit school in grade nine. He ended up finishing college with a Ph.D. in Engineering."

"I don't think I've ever been *that* wrong about a student," Barb said defensively.

"Maybe your students have just been living up to your low expectations."

Barb grimaced.

"The most important thing we can do for our students is offer them safe, caring classrooms where they have unlimited opportunities for learning. Where *they* decide, not *us,* how far they will go in life."

Barb's face relaxed a bit. "Okay, okay, I'll try working with him."

Jane smiled. "Barb, you're a great teacher."

"You're just trying to get me to live up to your expectations," Barb snickered.

Jane grinned. "When we feel good about ourselves, we're able to pass on those same good feelings to our students.

Chapter 28

Making Mistakes

Jane entered Peter Hopkins' classroom. The students were busily working on a written assignment. She wandered around looking at their work.

Fred, an eight-year-old boy with big black eyes, stood facing Peter as he sat at his desk.

"Fred, you can do better than this," Peter admonished him. "Look at this mess. I can barely read what you've written, and what I can read is trash."

Fred looked at his paper, despondent. Then wiped his misty eyes with the back of his hand.

Sasha came up to Peter's desk and stood behind Fred.

"Sasha, you've come up here and asked me about every little thing. Try it yourself first." Peter was annoyed.

Jane wandered over to Peter's desk.

Shaking his head in frustration, he said to her, "I wish they wouldn't keep asking me all those stupid questions. They don't even try."

"When Fred didn't do a good job, how did you make him feel?"

"But he's such a messy worker," Peter protested.

"At least he tried. If we create fear in our students for trying or for making mistakes, how can we expect them to risk learning?"

"We have to have standards," Peter stated adamantly.

"I agree, but kids learn from their mistakes. School needs to be a place where students feel safe enough to learn while making errors."

Peter looked skeptically at Jane, then at his class. Abruptly he stood up and marched over to Stewart's desk and grabbed a notebook from his lap. His eyes bored into Stewart's. "Cheating, huh?"

Stewart, a frail-looking seven-year-old, slumped his shoulders and stared glumly at his desk.

Peter checked the name on the notebook. "Tim, I want to speak with you *right now*!"

Tim's eyes went wide with fright.

Peter returned to his desk and faced Jane. "Well, what do you think of that?" He slammed the notebook down on his desk.

Jane approached Stewart. "Were you copying Tim's work?"

Stewart shrugged, his eyes remaining fixed on his pencil.

"Why were you copying his work?"

Stewart didn't answer. He stared at his lap.

"Do you understand how to do the assignment?" Jane asked.

Stewart shook his head.

Jane returned to Peter. "If Stewart doesn't know how to do the work, it's your job to explain it to him and help him get it right – without embarrassing him."

"Are you blaming me because *he* was cheating?" Peter was aghast.

"No. I just want you to understand that Stewart doesn't know how to do the work and needs your help, not your anger… only he's either too afraid or too embarrassed to ask you. He'd rather be bad than appear stupid."

Peter frowned.

"When students make mistakes or don't understand how to do the assignment, it's up to their teacher to work with them until they understand the lesson being taught. If our students aren't succeeding, then we aren't succeeding as teachers."

"I still don't condone cheating."

"Neither do I. But then you may need to create a classroom environment where there are no penalties for trying."

Peter rubbed his lower lip. "Is this part of that discovery process you talked about?"

Jane nodded, just as Fred returned to ask another question.

Peter grimaced and turned to Fred. "It doesn't matter if you get it wrong. Just try it on your own first."

Fred looked as if he was confused. "It's okay if I get it wrong?" He wanted to be sure he'd heard correctly.

Peter nodded, as he watched Fred's face light up.

Sasha wandered up again. Peter stopped her before she could ask her question. "Sasha, just try your best. We learn from our mistakes."

Sasha seemed uncertain as to what she should do. She looked at Jane, then back at Peter.

"It's okay. Just try." Peter smiled at her.

Sasha grinned and ran back to her desk.

Peter seemed perplexed by her reaction. He looked over at Stewart. "Bring your books up here and I'll help you."

Stewart's face and shoulders relaxed, as he rushed to gather up his books.

Peter turned to Tim, who had been waiting apprehensively beside him, and said, "If anyone needs help, it's my job, not yours, understand?"

Tim let his breath out in relief and eagerly nodded his head. He grabbed his notebook from Peter's desk and dashed back to his seat.

Peter surveyed his classroom. To Jane he said, "Can you believe it? They're smiling. I made them happy. I can't believe it."

Still shaking his head in disbelief, he announced, "Boys and girls, don't worry if you make any mistakes. We'll use those errors to learn from."

Little Patty, her black hair in a multitude of braids, put up her hand. "How many times can we erase?"

Peter smiled. "As many times as you need to."

The classroom began to feel lighter, brighter, as the children eagerly continued with their work. They had just learned that, in this classroom, it was okay to risk learning.

Chapter 29

That Inner Voice

Jody Goldstein was sitting in the teachers' lounge mumbling to herself as Jane came in to refill her coffee mug.

"What's the matter?" Jane asked.

"I'm just so mad at myself. I should've stayed home and worked last night. I can't believe I have so little will power."

"Where'd you go?"

"I went to see a movie. I don't know what's wrong with me. Sometimes I can't seem to motivate myself at night. I know I should be preparing lessons, but..."

"Jody, you've used some very powerful reprimands on yourself. Is it doing any good?"

"What do you mean?"

"By criticizing yourself, does that mean you'll choose differently next time?"

"I doubt it. If I have a chance to go out at night, I'll go. My teachers always told me I didn't have much common sense."

"Is it one of your teacher's voices reprimanding you in your head now?"

"You know, it sure sounds a lot like Miss Connor. She was always putting me down, telling me I couldn't do anything right. How did you know?"

"The words you're using are guilt words. Words we've heard

from our parents and teachers. You sound like you're just continuing to scold yourself in their absence."

"Oh?" Jody looked surprised.

"It seems to me as if last night you were choosing to do what you wanted to do, rather than what you thought you should be doing."

Jody nodded. "I think maybe you're right. I didn't want to work last night. I'm too tired at night, and if I work at home, I'm not fresh enough for the kids the next day. What am I going to do about it?"

"Why do you think you should be working at night?"

"My mom was a teacher. She always did. She told me it was the only way she could keep ahead of the kids."

"Is that true for you, too?"

"No, not really. I usually plan a whole unit at a time. I don't go day by day. I wouldn't know what I was doing if I did that."

"Then why reprimand yourself? Does it help you feel any better?"

"Oh no. I just have this voice in my head that's constantly telling me that I'm not good enough."

"Jody, you run a wonderful program, one of the best in this school. Your students are happy, their parents are complimentary. If your inner voice is sapping you of your self-esteem, you may need to reprogram that voice. Don't allow that voice to put you down. Stop it before it starts."

"I don't think it's as easy as you make it sound. Sometimes the voice is right. I can do stupid things."

"If you've made a mistake, try and see what you've learned from it and how that learning could be important to you. Reproaching yourself won't help you feel any better than it did when others criticized you."

"You know, I *have* been raised on a lot of negative programming."

"Many children are. Unfortunately, it can end up limiting their ability to learn and grow. And these same reprimands may continue to repeat themselves in a person's head well into adulthood."

Jody agreed. "My teachers always made me feel like I couldn't do anything right and my mom agreed with them. She was always nagging at me about something. And you know what? I'm better organized than she was. I don't have to work every night."

"Good. I'm glad to hear that."

"Wow! Parents really need to watch what they're saying to their children," Jody concluded.

"You're right. Both parents and teachers need to stop, or more important, never start programming their children with negative thoughts."

Jody nodded. "Our students really believe what we say to them about their abilities, don't they?"

"Yes, they do. We can help them to feel positive about themselves, or we can put them down. Either way, we can create a self-fulfilling prophecy."

Jody smiled. "I'm going to change my self-fulfilling prophecy."

"To what?" Jane asked.

"To one that says, I love helping my students learn and grow and I'm proud to be a part of this wonderful process. And… I'm really good at it."

"Right on!" Jane laughed.

Chapter 30

Kinesthetic Learning

The students worked quietly in Margaret Higgins' seventh grade classroom. Bobby Mendez sat at his desk, his foot tapping to a song in his head. He drummed his knee lightly with one hand and worked on his doodling with the other.

Margaret looked up from correcting papers at her desk. She stared at Bobby for a moment, trying to decide what punishment she should dole out to make him sit still.

Jane entered the room and handed Margaret a notice about the next staff meeting.

"What am I going to do about *him*?" Margaret pointed to Bobby.

"What's the problem?" Jane asked.

"He never stops moving."

"That's okay. He probably needs to move to learn."

"He's just doing it to annoy me. I'd give him another detention, but he already has three hours of detention left to serve from last week. I don't know what else to do with him. He can't do any of the work, he never pays attention. He needs to be in Special Education."

Jane surveyed the classroom as she listened. The classroom looked quite bare. There wasn't much information written on the blackboard or posted on the bulletin boards. "Do you like a very quiet classroom?" Jane asked.

"It's the only way if you want your students to be able to concentrate."

Some of the students were finishing up their work and beginning to put away their books.

"Will you be teaching another lesson soon?" Jane asked.

Margaret nodded. "History."

"Would you mind if I observed?"

Margaret got up from her desk and shrugged. "Suit yourself."

Jane watched as Margaret lectured her class on the Civil War. Some of her students listened intently, some made notes. Others moved restlessly in their seats, their minds elsewhere.

At the end of the lecture, Margaret told the class how to do their assignment. Several hands went up to have her repeat the instructions. Some students sounded like they had just returned from fantasyland and hadn't a clue what was going on. Bobby Mendez was one of them. When Bobby put up his hand to ask what he had to do after Margaret had already repeated the instructions twice, she yelled at him, "You never pay attention to anything that goes on in this classroom. I will not repeat myself again. Find out from someone else."

Margaret went back to her desk and sat down totally exasperated. "See what I mean. I don't know why I even bother to try." She threw up her hands.

"Bobby needs to learn kinesthetically," Jane stated.

"What does that mean?"

"It means he needs to learn by doing, by moving."

"I don't want a student to be constantly moving around. It drives me crazy."

"I can appreciate that. But being flexible is very important if you want to be able to reach all of the learners in your class. Our job is to help students learn in whatever way they need to."

"I do that. I tell them everything they need to know. But I still get half a dozen kids who always ask me to repeat myself." She shook her head, annoyed.

"Margaret, the students who are asking you to repeat yourself are the ones who don't learn best using only their ears to take in information. Some students need to either see the information or manipulate it in order to understand what you're talking about. By lecturing, you're only reaching the students who learn best auditorily. You're leaving out the other half of your class, who aren't comfortable learning in that way. Did you see all the kids who were fidgeting or staring off into space? How much of your lesson do you think they heard?"

"My job is to teach, their job is to learn."

"If you can't transfer the information to your students in a way that they're able to learn it, then you're wasting their time and yours."

"What am I supposed to be doing?"

"Creating lessons that take into account the different learning styles of your students."

"I have some students who do very well in my class," Margaret said defensively.

"I'm sure you do. Those are the students who learn well auditorily, just like you."

"I'm an auditory learner?"

"I think so. You have some of the signs. Your classroom has very little visual information posted. You enjoy lecturing. You're not comfortable working in a noisy environment."

Margaret agreed. "I need complete quiet or else I can't concentrate… but I thought everyone was like that."

"No, only some of the population. If you were a visual learner, you could probably study with the radio blaring and it wouldn't bother you."

"I can't even imagine that. How can I figure out which way my students learn best?" Margaret asked.

"Well, it's like this. Try to imagine each of your students has bought a new bicycle from the store. They get home and find out the bicycle needs assembling. The kinesthetic ones would just dive in and start working with the parts. The visual learners would read the instructions and then feel a bit better about putting it together. The auditory learners would call the company and ask what to do."

"That last part sure sounds like me. I guess I do prefer learning auditorily."

Jane smiled. "Auditory learners will usually say things like 'that sounds right.' Visual learners will say 'that looks right' and the kinesthetics, 'that feels right.' "

"Hmm, I'll have to pay closer attention and find out how my students prefer to learn. But back to programming. What do you suggest I do?"

"Create lessons that use all of the senses. Try using more written materials for your students who, if they can't see the information, don't understand it. Put the information on charts, use overheads, use mind maps. Anything so that these students can see what you're talking about as you're saying it. For the ones who need to move around, to take the information in through their bodies, offer them a chance to dramatize, build, manipulate, walk and talk about the information. Give them a chance to do whatever's necessary for them to internalize what you're trying to teach them. Take Bobby, for example. He can't learn if he's sitting still. Giving him detentions to teach him to sit still is only telling him that he's not okay, that his way of learning is wrong."

"What do you suggest he should do?"

"Have him work with a group of students to dramatize the Civil War. With his artistic ability, he could prepare the scenery, another student the script, others could play parts in the play. Anything to get your kinesthetic students moving and involved with the subject they're learning about."

"That's a great idea," Margaret's eyes lit up. "I'm going to try it right now."

"And if you're interested, I have lots of books in my office with all kinds of ideas for teaching different types of learners. You're welcome to borrow them."

Margaret smiled. "I'll do that."

Chapter 31

The Classroom Environment

The staff meeting started at four o'clock in the school library. Jane chaired the meeting. "In our last discovery meeting, we began by building a new level of safety and trust with each other. Can you tell me how we managed to do that?"

Fran put up her hand. "I know for me it was because we were allowed to be open and honest and everything we said was confidential. I could really be myself without worrying that if I said something wrong, I might lose my job. The confidentiality was very important to me."

Carole looked at Jane and said, "I started to see you as a safe person to be around, as someone I could tell my problems to. I felt I wouldn't be put down if I told you I was having problems with my class. You gave me some good suggestions. I tried them, and they've been working."

Jane smiled. "Thank you, that's very nice to hear."

Peter added, "I was really concerned that the last meeting was going to be our only meeting. I've seen too many ideas come and go that are never followed through. I like being a part of making changes. I don't like decisions handed down to me as a mandate. I like to learn by doing, and you're giving us a chance to do that."

Jane nodded in appreciation.

Jody added, "You're also being very supportive of us. You not only say positive things, but your body language agrees with your words. I didn't feel put down when we had our discussion. For me, you've become approachable. I like that."

Jane thanked Jody for her comments, and then uncovered a quote by Buckminster Fuller that she had written on a piece of chart paper. It said: "If you change the environment, you change the people."

Underneath, Jane had written a question: In your classroom, what are the perceived classroom values?

"I'd like each of you to reflect for a few moments on what is happening in your classroom, and what you wish were happening."

Several teachers looked disheartened.

Barb raised her hand. "What I believe I'm expecting is hard work, truthfulness, honesty, consideration of each other and respect for each other's personal property. But my students are certainly not living up to my expectations."

Margaret added, "Even if I discuss values in my classroom or tell my students that they're not working to their potential, it doesn't necessarily do any good or change their behavior."

"Good points," Jane responded. "Now, I want you to consider whether or not you feel you're modeling the behaviors and values you want your students to exhibit. Is there a match between what you're expecting from your students, and your own behavior?"

"Are you implying that we're irresponsible or rude?" Fran sounded annoyed.

"Our students can be a reflection of ourselves. If we don't like some of their behaviors, we may have to look at our own first."

"I don't know what you mean." Lillian was resistant.

"I'm asking that we check to make sure our behavior is consistent with what we're expecting from our students. If you ask your students to keep their desks tidy, and yours is always in a mess, what is the subconscious message? If students are being rude to each other, have they heard their teacher putting students down? If they have, then that teacher has told them that rude behavior is okay. If you make a promise to your students, do you keep it? Or do you always have a convenient excuse? Children are copycats. You cannot say to them, 'Do as I say, not as I do,' because they're learning how to act by modeling your behavior. We have to be very careful because many of our interactions with students have become so habitual, so subconscious, that we may not even be aware that we're sending out negative messages. With so much emphasis being placed on curriculum by the school district, we sometimes neglect to make sure we're creating an emotionally safe and consistent learning environment."

"We're loaded with new curriculums," Jody interrupted. "When are we supposed to have the time to spend creating environments?"

"Every interaction between teacher and student has the power to heal or to damage. Each moment we're in the classroom with our students we're creating the emotional environment. The question is, are we creating an environment where each student feels safe enough to risk learning, or are we creating an environment that's causing our students to shut down or rebel?"

The teachers were pensive.

"If you're having problems in your classroom, you may be the one who needs to change first," Jane continued. "Changing your approach may change the results."

"What do we change?" Lillian asked defensively.

"All the things that have helped you to feel safe in our meetings are what students need in order to feel safe in your classroom. They need honesty and openness, consistency, trust, integrity, support, a positive voice and encouraging body language. They need to know you're approachable, that they won't be put down, that you really care about them and their problems."

"What about academics?" Peter asked.

"Once you've created feelings of trust and safety with your students, they'll become willing learners, open to you and anything you want to teach them."

"What about the students who are behavior problems? Will they change, too?" Fran questioned.

"When you're feeling safe, and trust the environment you're in, do you have a need to misbehave?"

Fran thought about Jane's comment and shook her head.

The teachers looked at one another, uncertain at first about what they had just learned. Gradually they started moving their chairs closer together and began talking among themselves. Their language was supportive, their sharing moved to a deeper level.

Chapter 32

A Sharing Session

After the meeting Lillian approached Jane. "I was wondering if you could run a meeting. You know – a sharing session, with my class. I'm not sure if I can do it."

"I'd be glad to." Jane smiled.

"Good. How about tomorrow morning?"

"I'll be there."

Jane was at Lillian's fourth grade classroom door the next morning, just as the bell rang.

As the students entered the classroom, Jane greeted each with a personal question or compliment. Some students responded, others looked strangely at her as if to say, what's with you?

Jane held the attendance folder and called out the list of names, again connecting personally with every student. She either made a personal comment, or wished them a good morning.

When she was finished, Jane surveyed the expectant faces of the students while Lillian sat unobtrusively at her desk watching. "Boys and girls, I've heard from Miss Campbell that you're a great class, one of the best she's ever had."

Some students giggled, others sat up straighter as they listened.

"We're going to be doing some interesting new things this morning and I want you to know how excited I am to have this opportunity to be here with you. This is going to be a great day.

"I would like us all to gather in a circle at the back of the room. I would like each of you to be comfortable. If you want you can sit on the floor, or if you prefer you can bring a chair. Please assemble now."

Wesley put up his hand. "What are we going to do?"

"We're going to get to know each other a little better."

"I'll pass," Wesley stated.

Lillian walked over to Wesley's desk and was about to order him to participate when Jane interrupted, "No, it's okay."

Lillian gave Wesley a dirty look and started to go back to her desk.

"Please join us?" Jane invited Lillian.

She looked uncertain, but picked up her chair and joined the group.

Jane returned her attention to Wesley. "Is there a problem?"

"I just don't like that kind of thing."

"I would like you to join us, but if you don't want to now, you can watch what we're doing from your desk and, if you'd like to join us later, that's fine."

"I won't."

"Then I would ask you to please not disturb the rest of the class while we're working. Okay?"

Wesley nodded, pulled a book out of his desk, opened it and feigned reading.

Jane headed to the back of the room. The students had assembled in a circle. They had saved a chair for her.

"Thank you," Jane smiled as she sat down. "Miss Campbell invited me into your classroom this morning to give us a chance to get to know each other better. There are a lot of students whom I interact with in this school, but some I never have the opportunity to get to know very well. Today is our chance to find out more about each other. Before we start, I want to go over some suggestions for sharing that I hope will help us all feel more comfortable."

Navneet, a cute ten-year-old with long black braids, put up her hand. "Do we have to write this stuff down?" She wrinkled her nose at the thought.

Jane smiled. "No, we're here to listen and to share our experiences."

Navneet nodded and crossed her legs on the floor to make herself more comfortable.

Jane began, "My first suggestion is that when we speak, we only talk about ourselves and our experiences. We forget about gossiping or blaming."

The students nodded in agreement. Jane continued, "And whatever we say here is completely confidential. We're not to talk about people behind their backs. I would like whatever we hear in this room to stay in this room. Is there anybody in this group who doesn't feel that they can follow either of these suggestions?"

No one raised a hand. Wesley was looking toward the group with interest.

"To help us get started, I've made this paper heart. Written on it is 'Speaking from the Heart.' When you have the heart in your hand, it's your turn to talk. We'll pass the heart around and when you have it you may speak, ask questions, share, or pass it on to the next person. You aren't required to say anything if you don't wish to. I only ask that when one person is sharing, the rest of you are listening. Is there anyone here who feels they cannot do that?" Jane asked.

The class was silent.

"Good. Since we'll each have a chance to share, is there any topic you'd like us to talk about to help you get to know the people in your class better?"

Candice, a stout blond girl, said with a lisp, "I'd like to know what people's hobbies are."

"That's a good suggestion. Any others?"

Thomas, a child with big, expressive brown eyes put up his hand. "I'd like to know what pets people have."

"Another good suggestion. Damian?"

Damian was big and gawky. He shifted in his seat, then said, "I'd like to know what sports people play, and if they play on teams."

"Good. Those are three good suggestions. You may want to share using one of those three questions as a guideline, or you may want to share other information that's important to you. I'd like to start off this session, if that's okay with the class?"

The students nodded their consent.

"I've always loved animals and when I was young I had a cat, named Fluffer. He was a white Angora cat with a spot of black fur on his tummy. He knew me so well, I was sure he could read my mind."

Jane told the students about some of the funny things Fluffer did, like getting all tangled up in a ball of yarn until he couldn't move. She told them how Fluffer once climbed up the living room drapes and jumped onto a hanging light fixture. He was so afraid to come down that Jane had to get a ladder to rescue him. Then she told the students how sad and lost she felt when her cat died after she'd had him for sixteen years. The students listened, and asked her questions about her sad feelings.

The "heart" went around the room. Students chose to either share or just listen. The sharing was simple. The students asked questions and listened intently. Jane thanked each student for participating. After a while, the students also started thanking each other for sharing. Wesley came to join the group. He wanted to tell about his team's basketball victory.

At the end of the session, Jane asked each student to share what they felt they had learned from this experience, and how they might use this experience to help them in the future.

The feedback was positive. The students had enjoyed getting to know each other better and felt they had become closer friends.

Chapter 33

Not Convinced

Jane was satisfied with their first session. The students had been relaxed and had participated willingly. There had not been many interruptions.

Afterward, Lillian took Jane aside. "I don't see how sharing is going to make any difference in my classroom. It's not going to help them get better grades. It's a waste of time."

"How did you feel after you had shared?"

Lillian thought about it for a moment and then shrugged. "It was okay. The students seemed to care about what I said. Losing my parakeet doesn't sound like much, but it meant a lot to me."

"The students seemed to know how you felt. A lot of them have suffered similar losses. I don't think it matters what kind of pet we lose, our love for them is just as real. Sharing keeps us from feeling different or alone with our feelings. We learn that we've all shared similar experiences and emotions."

"A number of the kids seemed to have liked the sharing, but they're the same ones that always like to talk. Those kids don't need an excuse like a sharing session."

Jane nodded. "Some of the students who didn't share may need time to feel safe with the process. They need to become comfortable with speaking in front of the group."

Lillian pursed her lips, as if she was still not convinced. "Well, thanks for trying." She turned away.

"I'd like you to run the next session."

"Oh, I don't know about that. I'm not comfortable doing those kinds of things. It's not my style of teaching. This touchy-feely stuff, it's not for me. I'll stick to my way of doing things. I'm not looking for problems."

"By sharing, you're creating an atmosphere of trust and caring. If problems arise, it gives you and your students a chance to deal with them, to understand the real issues. Through sharing, students will start to realize they're responsible for their own actions and can discover ways of resolving conflicts both with their peers and with the adults in their lives."

"I would be giving up too much control."

"You're not giving up anything. You're moving from a position of control to one of cooperation. Your students will begin to listen to one another, to get to know each other better, to cooperate with you and their peers."

"I don't see how that can happen by talking about pets!"

"At first some of their sharing may sound superficial, but eventually, as your students start to feel safe with the process, they'll begin to share on much deeper levels. Then, as problems surface, students can deal with the issues and discuss them in a non-threatening manner. It can lead to a greater understanding of themselves and others."

"I don't see how that would ever happen. I think you're expecting an awful lot from fourth graders."

Jane disagreed. "Once your students begin to experience your relationship with them as being trusting and caring, they'll start to respond to you and their classmates in the same way."

"That would be nice," Lillian said, "but I still think you're dreaming."

"If you would like to run the sharing meeting tomorrow morning, I can be there to help you."

"What would I have to do?"

"Share a piece of yourself. Show genuine respect and interest in your students. Invite them to be real with you. Create a safe environment for you and your students to relate in."

Lillian looked uncertain. "I don't know. They'll bicker and fight. I know them. As soon as they think I've gone soft on them, they'll start. Besides, they always want to sit beside their friends and act silly, especially Wesley."

"We all want to sit beside people who like us. We're social beings. We like to be part of a group that accepts us. Don't you sit with your friends at staff meetings?"

"I guess I do," Lillian realized.

"It's part of our nature. Just remember not to use fear or guilt to get the students to participate. Use an approachable voice to invite them to the sharing session. If you push them, you'll find they push back, and the whole process will lose its trusting, caring quality. If your students are acting silly or have a problem, listen non-judgmentally to what they have to say about their behavior. Find out what you can agree with. Appreciate their honesty. Then work toward resolving the issues. Turn it into a win-win situation. Getting the last word is not important."

"Then I *am* giving up control of my students."

"No, you're finding a different way to be with them. You're taking the time to understand their world, from their point of view, instead of trying to sell them on your view of life. You're expanding your world to include theirs."

Lillian seemed to have that doubtful look on her face again.

"Isn't that how you'd like to be treated if you had a problem?" Jane asked.

Lillian thought about it for a moment. "I suppose so."

"When we teach through control, we're using a lot of our own energy to run things. When there's cooperation, everyone is using their energy to help make the classroom experience great."

"School was never like that when I went to school."

"Did you like school?"

"I lived through it. When I went into teaching, I never thought I'd end up coddling the kids. I teach them as I was taught. Obey the rules and respect your teachers. But the kids today, you have to keep at them all the time. They never show any respect."

"I remember when I went to school," Jane said, "it wasn't a happy time for me. If I didn't think the teacher cared about me, I didn't do very well. I don't think kids today are much different."

"My favorite teacher always picked me to erase the blackboard. All the kids were jealous of me," Lillian reminisced.

"She made you feel special."

"I did really well that year, probably my best year."

"Let's try and make every year, for all students, their best year. If all children know they're special, think about how much better their grades will be."

"Okay, I'll try it. But what should we talk about?"

"You could ask them to talk about their special gifts or talents. You could try asking them to share a happy experience, or a sad time in their lives, or a time of loneliness. You could ask them to share ways in which they've changed over the last few years, and what events have caused the changes in their lives. Or better still, ask the students what they'd like to share. There may be issues they want to discuss. There are so many things we don't know about our students that could help us to empathize and relate to them better."

"I've always kept my emotions to myself," Lillian admitted. "I don't want anyone to know what I'm feeling. This isn't easy for me."

"Learning to share when we've never done it before isn't easy. Sometimes we just feel more comfortable sharing successes, not disappointments."

"When I feel hurt, I don't want to talk about it."

"I understand. But those are the times it's most important for us to share, to know that people still care about us."

Lillian grimaced. She still was not convinced.

Chapter 34

New Rules

Each student in Carole's Special Education class had a learning problem and had been declared learning disabled. The students were in this class to receive special programming to help them overcome their difficulties.

As Jane entered the room, she observed that each student was busy at a work station. Some were working on math, others on the computer, some on a project about their country.

Posted on the front bulletin board were the new classroom rules. There were only three. Be polite; Don't take other people's things; Remember to bring back your homework each morning.

Carole wandered over to where Jane was reading the list. "I got each student to initial beside each rule to show that they agreed with it and were willing to abide by it."

"Great idea," Jane grinned, "and I see it seems to be working." She gestured toward the students who were diligently completing their tasks.

"I was surprised at first, but it is," admitted Carole. "It seems that because they now feel a part of creating what's happening in the classroom, they're more willing to participate in a positive way. Their behavior has really improved."

"By respecting and empowering your students, they in turn, are respecting you."

"I guess so. I was so afraid at first of letting go. But you were right, what I was doing wasn't working anyway, so why hang on to it."

"I'm glad. How are the students doing academically?"

"Well, I've been trying a few new things with them since we started those discovery meetings. We have sharing sessions at the end of each day. I ask my students how their day was. What did they like about it? What would they like to change? What was great? What wasn't? What did they learn? What do they want more of? What needs to be clarified? It's been wonderful. I've gained valuable insights into my students that have really helped me to improve my program. I feel like I'm now meeting my students' needs and they love it. I never have any behavior problems with them when we're sharing. Joe, over there," Carole pointed to a student wearing a striped yellow shirt, "told me he feels in control of his learning now, and he's doing great. He's not being rude or belligerent anymore."

"This is great news. I'm so glad the students know how much you really care about them. I hope you'll share what you're doing with the other teachers."

"They can even come in and observe if they want to."

Jane was thrilled.

Chapter 35

Modeling Our Leaders

Jane hung up the phone. Talking with Sarah brought back such wonderful memories. Sarah was as excited as Jane about all the great changes that were starting to be a part of East County Elementary School.

As Jane leafed through the beautiful pictures of her trip that she had just received in the mail from Sarah, the phone rang again.

"Hi Bill, what's up?"

Bill was calling with an invitation for Jane's seventh graders to visit East County Junior High.

"I'm sure they'd love to hear the Chairman of the County Commission speak. What time is Mr. Jefferson going to be at your school?"

He told her it had been arranged for two o'clock that afternoon.

Jane hesitated. It was short notice, but the experience would be great for the kids. "We'll be there." Jane said good-by to Bill and hurried to Margaret Higgins' room.

The seventh graders sat politely in the East County Junior High School auditorium and listened to Mr. Jefferson, a tall slim man in his forties, with slick dark hair. The Chairman stood on the stage and leaned on the podium as he talked about his administration. He told the students about the problems the county was facing, and blamed the last administration for contributing to all of his woes. He criticized them for not balancing the budget, and for getting the county deeper into debt.

Jane stood at the back of the auditorium with Bill.

"Terrific speaker, isn't he?" Bill said, obviously proud he had been able to bring such a prominent speaker to his school.

"He may be a great speaker, but he's a poor role model," Jane answered.

"What do you mean? Look at all he's done, and getting into office is a big achievement."

"We're trying to teach our students to be responsible for their own actions. I haven't heard one statement from him where he has taken any responsibility for what his office is doing. He's telling us his problems and totally blaming his inability to do anything about them on the last administration. So, in effect, he's telling our kids, if at first you don't succeed, blame someone. I didn't vote him into office to spend his time telling me why he can't achieve his goals. I voted him in to make changes. It was a waste of a vote," Jane said, annoyed.

"You're overreacting. Calm down." Bill seemed surprised by her comments.

"When your students do something wrong and won't take responsibility for their actions, just remember that they're copying the leaders of this society. If our own leaders are choosing to avoid accountability by relying on blame as an acceptable excuse, how can we expect our students to show any different kind of behavior?"

Bill was silent for a moment, then he walked up to the stage.

"Mr. Jefferson." Bill stopped him in mid-sentence.

Mr. Jefferson looked at Bill, visibly annoyed by the interruption. "Yes?" There was an irritated edge to his voice.

"I asked you to come here to speak to my students to present a positive role model for them. You've spent the last half hour blaming your predecessors. The kids already know how to blame everyone around them. They already know how to shirk their responsibilities. They don't need any more lessons or justification for their actions. I would appreciate it if you would close off your speech right now."

Jane started applauding. The students turned and looked at her, confused at first, then they too started applauding.

Mr. Jefferson mumbled something from the podium that could not be heard over the clapping, and quickly left the stage.

Jane walked up to Bill. "Bravo! I knew you had it in you."

Bill looked as if he was a little shaken by what he had just done. He took a deep breath to center himself and then began to ask his teachers to clear the auditorium.

Jane interrupted him. "Bill, don't throw away this great learning opportunity. Discuss what just happened with the students. This is a wonderful chance to open up a dialogue on responsibility. Don't waste it."

Bill immediately shifted gears and went up on stage to conduct the discussion himself.

Chapter 36

Evaluating Students

Jane and her teachers had gathered in the school library to discuss evaluating students. In the notice Jane had sent around, she stated that it was part of their school's discovery process. The teachers had been a little perplexed. A report card was a report card. What did she have in mind now?

Bill Carson had decided to join the meeting and sat with the others at one of the library's round tables. Bill had been impressed by Jane's insights with regards to Mr. Jefferson, and discussions with Jane afterward led him to concede that she might be onto something. He was still being noncommittal, but said he would observe and take notes.

Jane had a piece of chart paper posted at the front of the room. On it were three questions for her staff to consider:

1. Do student evaluations require some students to do less well in order to distinguish those who do better?
2. Are students encouraged to support one another's learning, or are they encouraged only to compete with each other?
3. Do some students get the feeling that their value as a human being and their ability to know how well they are doing in life comes from comparing themselves and from being compared to others?

Bill appeared to be surprised by the depth of the questions. Jane knew that although he had been a principal a long time, he had never thought to challenge the way students were evaluated. He had always felt standardized report cards were important to be able to compare how students were doing across the country. But these three questions seemed to create some conflicts in his thinking. Jane knew that school district bureaucrats were always talking about building self-esteem in students. But teachers were still subjecting students to harsh evaluations in report cards, telling students that they're not good enough or failures compared to their peers. The system was in contradiction with itself.

"I hope you've had enough time to consider these three questions," Jane said to her staff. "Since it's our job as teachers to empower our students by helping them discover their individual self-worth, I question whether our present methods of evaluating them do this. I believe it's disempowering for students to believe that if they're not getting grades as good as the person next to them, they're not as valuable a human being."

Fran interrupted. "We don't ever say that to our students. But we need to give them grades and we can't help it if some students do better work than others."

"I agree with you. We often don't say that in words, but many times we imply it through our actions, and that can be just as detrimental. I feel that to empower our students we must make sure our evaluations are not creating disillusionment and failure, but offering students the kind of feedback and support they need to help them become better at what they're doing."

Margaret raised her hand. "Isn't learning to accept failure part of the learning process?"

"You're right, we learn by trial and error. It's hard to find a successful person who hasn't experienced failure, and lots of it. But, unfortunately, in school, failure has such a strong negative meaning that it prevents many students from risking learning. We need students to feel it's okay to try and not be afraid of failure – to understand that failure just means you haven't found the solution yet. If you're not afraid to fail, then you're more likely to keep trying until you succeed."

Peter interrupted, "I remember when I went to school, failure meant humiliation and ridicule, even from your best friends. It can be a very painful experience."

Jane nodded. "Thank you, Peter, for sharing that."

Margaret added, "I remember I never knew what failure was until I went to school. My kindergarten teacher made me feel so bad because I kept putting my shoes on the wrong feet. She never once complimented me on how well I tied them, most of the kids couldn't even do that. But she used to make me feel stupid because I couldn't tell my two shoes apart. I felt like such a failure. Oh, I can't believe how angry it makes me feel even today, thirty years later."

"It's unfortunate that those feelings of failure, of never being good enough, stay with us for life," Jane acknowledged.

"What are you suggesting we do?" Bill asked.

"I'd like to see report cards offering constructive information with regards to the goals and objectives set out for each student. I'd like students to be aware of their own progress and be able to chart their own successes. I believe it's very important for every student to feel that there's positive movement forward."

"How do you propose the teacher come up with all these individual goals? That's a lot of work." Bill shook his head.

"Bill, before I answer that, let me ask you some questions first. How many kids see themselves as victims, as people that life happens to?"

"Lots."

"How many kids make poor choices in life?"

"Too many," Bill conceded.

"How many students feel they don't know where they're going, or how they're going to get there?"

"Most of them."

"If things are happening to kids, then they're victims and are not in control of their destiny. What we need to do is help our students take control over what's happening to them. Help them become empowered decision-makers. And we can do this by teaching our students how to set personal and academic goals."

"You want the students to set the goals?" Bill looked surprised.

"Students working with their teachers can learn how to set goals. It's an important skill that everyone needs in life. It means learning how to evaluate where you are now, where you want to be and how you're going to get there. It's learning when and how to correct your course of action. These are all important skills our students need. If we don't teach them how to do that, then their destiny becomes something that happens *to* them, not something they've *created.*"

"Are you suggesting students evaluate their own work?" Bill asked skeptically.

"When students are not a part of their own evaluations, they're giving over their personal power to someone else. That's a powerless position. Our goal is to help shift students from being powerless to being powerful."

Bill slowly nodded his head in agreement.

Jane continued, "We're all unique, and when students become aware of their own uniqueness, then they'll know how foolish it is to compare themselves to anyone else, or to allow someone else to compare them to another. It's very important for students to be able to accept themselves just as they are right now. Part of developing self-confidence and self-esteem is not letting what happens outside of you define who you are."

Jody raised her hand. "What you're saying is true for teachers, too. Just listening to you talk, I realize how often I've defined myself based on what other people have said about me or on how they've acted toward me. Now I understand I was giving away my power and letting others define who I am. I feel this is a very valuable insight for me. Thank you for sharing it."

Jane smiled in appreciation.

"Will students still fail their grade if they can't do the work?" Lillian asked.

"If students are a part of their own evaluation process, then it makes sense for them to take part in that decision, too. They know if they're ready to move ahead or not. When students are responsible for their own progress, our position becomes one of advisor, not judge."

Bill grinned at Jane. "You really are quite an agent of change. You know, I wish things had been like this when I went to school. I think I would have done a lot better. I'd like you to help me make some changes in my school. And you know what? I think I'll give Clayton Tarelton at East County High School a call. I think he should be in on this too."

Jane felt elated.

Chapter 37

A Gift

The clock on the wall said five-thirty. Jane gathered up her papers and put them into her briefcase. There was a light knock on her office door. She looked up. Charlie stood in the doorway, laughing.

Jane jumped up and exclaimed, "What are you doing here?"

"Sarah told me about the wonderful work you've been doing, so I brought you something."

Charlie took her hand and led her to the outer office. There was a rocking chair made out of maple wood, just like Sarah's!

Jane's eyes went wide with delight. "Oh, Charlie!"

"Where shall I put it?" he asked.

"In there." Jane pointed excitedly to her office and followed Charlie in. She sat in her new chair and gently rocked. "I love it! Thank you so much."

"Thank Sarah, too."

"Sarah?"

Sarah appeared in the doorway. Jane rushed up and hugged her.

"We got here about an hour ago," Sarah explained. "We were standing outside the library during your meeting. You were wonderful."

"Sarah, I can't thank you enough for all you've taught me. I feel like I'm finally doing what I was meant to do. My school is starting to become a place where students aren't afraid of being themselves. They're beginning to risk discovering their potential. It's so exciting!"

Chapter 38

High School

Clayton Tarelton, the principal of East County High School, escorted Jane to the high school's staff meeting in the school library. Clayton was a heavy-set man in his late forties.

As they headed down the hall, Clayton remarked, "When Bill first called me and told me what he was going to do in his school and that he thought I should try it here, I figured he was crazy. You know the old adage, 'You can't change the system, you can't change the kids.'"

Jane nodded.

"But you know, after working with Gretchen, who I was sure would either end up failing, dropping out, getting pregnant, or all of those things, I am amazed. I can't believe how two teachers could create such different results."

Jane remembered her first meeting with Clayton. Almost immediately he was called away to deal with Gretchen. She had skipped class again and was discovered behind the school with several rough-looking guys.

As Jane later learned, Gretchen's parents were divorcing and Gretchen wasn't handling it very well. Each day her father would drop her off in front of the school, but Gretchen seldom made it into the building. Although she had once been tested and was found to be intellectually very bright, she was failing miserably. It was doubtful she would pass tenth grade. Whenever she did make it to class, she made life difficult for everyone. Her work was never complete, she was argumentative and disruptive, annoying her teachers and all those sitting around her.

After speaking with Jane, Clayton had decided to have a meeting with all of Gretchen's teachers. He explained to them that Gretchen was a very troubled student. She wasn't taking her parent's divorce very well and needed a lot of emotional support.

Her science teacher, Mr. Cormley, had said he would not treat her any differently. If she didn't do her work, she would fail. That was it. He was there to teach and it was her job to learn. And if she didn't, there wasn't much he would do about it. He had too many kids in his classes who wanted to learn, for him to waste his time worrying about a troublemaker like her.

On the other hand, Mrs. Rivera, Gretchen's English teacher, opened her heart to her. She made her feel welcomed and cared for in her classroom. She called her at home to tell her when she did well on an assignment. She encouraged her to write and keep a journal of her thoughts and ideas. She made time for Gretchen to share those ideas with her. She listened and cared about Gretchen's problems and her life. Gretchen went from a failing grade in English at mid-term, to a B plus.

Mr. Cormley refused to see Gretchen as anything other than a disruptive nuisance. She eventually dropped out of science. Gretchen's only comment was, "It didn't seem to matter how hard I tried. I couldn't please Mr. Cormley."

What a difference a teacher could make, Jane thought.

Clayton continued, "Do you remember we talked about Robert Farling? He was one of our Special Education graduates."

Jane nodded.

"Well, he came in to see me again the other day. He still hasn't found a job. I'm afraid he's going to end up on welfare. His self-esteem is so low. He's gone for a few job interviews and didn't get anything; now he's afraid to even apply. I always thought he had good potential, but I guess we never relayed that message to him."

"That's too bad."

"Unfortunately I think we've made a similar mistake with Calvin."

Jane looked at Clayton. "Oh?"

"Mr. Matini, the guidance counselor, gave Cal a career aptitude test. Cal loved to work on all kinds of machines. But after the test, Mr. Matini told him he would never make it as a mechanic. He told him to become a cook. I think it really confused Cal. He liked to cook, but he loved to work on cars. He would go down to the auto shop and tinker with cars whenever he had a spare class. He kept insisting he wanted to be a mechanic, but Mr. Matini told him he didn't stand a chance at getting his mechanic's papers. Cal got so discouraged, his marks dropped. Now he's gone and quit school."

Jane winced.

"We didn't understand kinesthetic students," said Clayton. "I didn't know they rarely do well on tests. We completely missed how well he worked with his hands and we scared him away from becoming a mechanic. We made him think he wasn't bright enough to succeed. There have to be some changes made around here. Our students need to know we believe in them."

"What's Cal doing now?" Jane asked.

"I'm not sure."

"Did you ever think of inviting him back to finish high school? Help him succeed. Teach him what he needs to know to get his mechanic's papers."

Clayton nodded. "Good idea, I'll see if I can get in touch with him. His brother still goes to school here."

As they turned the corner toward the library, Marcia Gilbert, a twelfth grade math teacher, joined them. "Clayton, I've just had a visit from David Ross."

"How's he doing?" Clayton asked and then turned to Jane. "All his teachers used to complain that he was really distractible. Turns out, he was bored. He just got accepted to college based on his entrance exam."

Marcia added, "At first I couldn't believe it. He hardly did any of the work. I thought he couldn't."

Jane smiled, "It's sometimes hard to tell the difference between a slow student and a bored one. When students are uninspired, they may only be doing the absolute minimum they need to do to get by."

Clayton entered the library and turned to Jane. "So what will you be sharing with us today?"

"How about awakening each student's inner brilliance?"

Chapter 39

Brilliance Awakening

Jane sat in her rocking chair and reflected on her first year as principal. She thought about all the students in her school who had started to blossom.

There was Bobby Mendez, the boy who couldn't sit still. He ended up organizing a drama production of the Civil War that he not only put on for his class, but for the whole school. He was then invited to Bill's junior high school to put on the play for the older students. Bobby had become excited about learning. Margaret no longer thought he belonged in Special Education, or expected him to sit still. He was encouraged to dramatize, build and produce, to do whatever he needed to do, to learn. He was going to pass his year. He was very excited about going to East County Junior High; there he was already a rising star in the eyes of the students.

She hadn't seen Gordon in a long time. Barb had done a wonderful job of creating a positive rapport with him. Once Barb took the time to look inside herself, she remembered that she had become a teacher because she loved kids. She no longer made excuses, but sought solutions to the difficulties she was having with her students. She showed Gordon she cared about him, and she really did. She would boost his self-esteem by talking positively to him, and by giving him more and more responsibility in the classroom. He had a real knack for getting things done, and done well. But most of all, Barb gave Gordon her time. She became sensitive to his needs. She knew instinctively when he had a problem and when he needed someone to talk to. She would sit and listen and let him know she cared. Gordon learned that he no longer needed to strike out at the other students to get the attention he needed. He was learning to ask Barb to sit and talk. He still had problems at home, but he had become a model student.

Lillian had never become comfortable with running the sharing meetings, so Wesley had stepped in and taken over. He was such a likable young man that the students gravitated toward him and respected his leadership.

Sasha's mother called yesterday. She wanted to tell Jane that Sasha loved going to school and asked if Peter could teach third grade next year, so that Sasha could have him again as her teacher. Peter had decided that trying to be in control of everything in his classroom was creating too many stress lines on his face. He was now working on creating a harmonious classroom with set sharing times at the beginning of each day. He told Jane last week that he wished his teachers had built him up when he went to school. He had always been rather timid and for the first time, since the sharing sessions had started in his class, he was beginning to feel comfortable with himself. He told her how much he loved teaching now and was sorry he had to retire in five years. He had even begun to throw out his outdated teaching materials and was looking at new ways to make his program fresh and exciting.

Jane picked up the new student handbook. It was ready for the new school year. The Student Rules Committee had eliminated all of the old rules and created five new ones. Jane felt a sense of pride as she read them:

1. Speak to others as you would want them to talk to you. If you say something nice to someone, it makes you feel good, too.

2. It's okay to fail; it's not okay not to try.
3. Don't compare yourself to anyone. Believe in yourself.
4. Blaming makes you a victim. Be responsible for your own actions.
5. If you're not happy with someone, changing your approach may change their attitude.

Jane put down the book. The students were certainly very wise. Carole's Special Education class had played a big role in creating the new rules.

The behavior in Carole's class had changed dramatically when Carole was finally able to let go of the control. By offering her students the opportunity to decide what rules they needed in their classroom, and by giving them the chance to give her input on their learning program, her students had gone from feeling powerless to powerful. They no longer needed to misbehave; the classroom program was meeting their needs. Carole had invited several of the other teachers in to observe her end-of-day sharing sessions. Fran and Jody had ended up duplicating her sharing program in their own classrooms.

Fran had even initiated relaxation sessions with her students. She played soothing classical music while the students sat comfortably anywhere they pleased. Fran would then gently talk them into a peaceful state by telling them to relax their muscles and quiet their minds. She found it was wonderful for increasing her students' concentration. Their behavior and academic performance had also improved. Each day her students eagerly looked forward to their fifteen-minute relaxation break.

The toxic talk from her staff had all but disappeared. Her teachers had begun to realize their own value as both teachers and human beings; they were becoming exciting, energizing people to be around.

Bill Carson and Clayton Tarelton were implementing changes in their schools, too. Many of their teachers were reluctant, but progress had been steady. Jane had been spending as much time as possible in their schools to help them create the necessary changes. When her students reached junior high and then high school, she wanted them to feel as accepted and as cared for as they did at East County Elementary.

Jane remembered the stories about students who didn't feel they belonged. They were the ones who had joined gangs, did drugs, committed crimes and sometimes even tried suicide. Jane hoped that the feelings of belonging and caring, that were beginning to permeate her school, would mean she would never read about any of her students being accused of any wrongdoing.

There was a knock on her office door.

"Come in," Jane called.

The door opened and to her surprise, her entire teaching staff walked in. Fran was carrying a package in her hand.

Barb stepped forward. "Jane, we want to thank you for an exciting and enlightening school year. As this was only your first year as principal, we wanted you to know how much we've enjoyed working with you and that the gift we have for you expresses what we believe is your destiny."

Fran presented Jane with the package, which was covered with floral wrapping paper and tied with a big red ribbon.

Jane was so surprised, she could barely keep her hands from shaking as she opened it.

Inside was a bronze plaque. Written on it were the words: To a Great Principal. It was signed by all of her teachers.

Peter spoke up, "I've been a teacher for a long time and you're by far the best principal I've ever worked for. You've made a big difference in the lives of your teachers and in the lives of your students. I'm proud to have had a chance to work with you. Thank you."

Tears of joy welled in Jane's eyes as each of the teachers approached her and gave her a big hug.

"We're just like one big, happy family," Carole exclaimed, as the teachers began to hug each other.

Chapter 40

The Voyage Continues

The summer sun was hot and humid. Jane looked out at the clear, calm ocean of the Florida Keys and rocked lazily in Sarah's chair. Sarah came out of her house carrying a tray. On it was a pitcher of iced tea and some glasses. She placed the tray on the table and sat down on the porch swing.

"Sarah, I owe it all to you. It was destiny meeting you."

"There's always a reason when paths cross. We've learned a lot from each other."

Jane was surprised. "What did you learn from me?"

"I learned that anything is possible, if we want it badly enough. You're quite a principal."

"Thank you, you're a great teacher," Jane smiled, "but I have some teachers in my school who one day may challenge you for your title."

Sarah leaned back on the swing. "I'm really glad to hear that. One day I hope every teacher will be great. It would make school just what it should be, a wonderful place for students to become proud of who they are. A place where they broaden their horizons in classrooms meant for limitless learning and discovering their brilliance."

"It sure sounds wonderful to me." Charlie turned the corner of the house and stepped onto the porch.

"Eavesdropping, were you?" Jane laughed.

Charlie grinned at her. "I'd like school to be an inspiring place for all students, since they have to be there anyway," he added.

"Destiny is a funny thing," Sarah said. "If Jane's jet-ski hadn't drifted so close to my home and you hadn't saved her and brought her here, all of our lives would have been very different. We would never have had the opportunity to touch each other's lives so profoundly. We've helped each other learn and grow."

Jane looked at Sarah and Charlie with a peaceful smile. "And as each of us grows, recognizing our own uniqueness and self-worth, we become empowered to change the world."

Epilogue

"If you treat students the way they are, you never improve them. If you treat them the way you want them to be, you do."
— J. W. von Goethe

Educators have been entrusted with the most important profession in the universe.

When teachers believe if the student is not learning it's a problem with the student, rather than with the teaching system, they may be creating a Walter Hunt. Most people don't know who Walter Hunt was.

Walter Hunt was responsible for more inventions than almost any other American who ever lived. He invented the fountain pen, rifle, sewing machine, and burglar and fire alarms. Yet he died in poverty in 1796. Although Walter Hunt's brilliant mind could have made him rich and famous, he died broke and disillusioned. Why? Because for all his genius, he lacked belief in himself and his ideas. You may have a Walter Hunt in your classroom.

As teachers, every positive interaction, thought and feeling contributes to creating a better world. As Henry B. Adams wisely said back in 1918, "A teacher affects eternity."

LOVE, CARE AND SHARE WITH YOUR STUDENTS – OUR FUTURE DEPENDS ON THEM

APPENDIX A

"In a completely rational society, the best of us would aspire to be teachers, and the rest would settle for something less, because passing civilization along from one generation to the next ought to be the highest honor and the highest responsibility anyone could have."

— Lee Iacocca

1. Creating Harmonious Classrooms

Creating immediate teacher-student rapport:

1. Greet students at the door with a "good morning" and a personal question or compliment.
2. As you are taking attendance, again, connect personally with each student.
3. Tell the students that they're a great class and how excited you are to be their teacher.
4. Let the students know that this is going to be a great day.
5. Use positive verbal suggestions and positive body language to create an environment where students are happy to be and feel safe from the fear of put-downs.

Creating the physical environment:

- Ideally, the room should have a rug, flowers or plants and music to help create a positive and happy atmosphere.

- Desks and learning centers should be movable to allow for flexible seating – have students sit on the floor, on chairs, on pillows.
- Post positive signs to encourage and inspire students, such as:
  "I can do it!"
  "I've decided to have a great day!"
  "I'm feeling energized!"
  "I'm a positive friend."
  "It's safe to make a mistake here."
  "Say something nice to someone and feel good too."
  "It's okay to risk learning in this classroom."
  "To have a friend, be a friend."
  "Every little step I take, is a step toward my success."
  "I'm proud to be me."
  "It's safe to be yourself here."

Creating great energy in the classroom:

- Create lessons that take into account the different learning styles of each student. Lessons should inspire a sense of curiosity, interest and excitement.
- Present classroom material in a variety of formats, such as: demonstrations, guest speakers, hands-on practice, experiments, mechanical instruction, computers and model building. Use games to defocus the learning process and produce stress-free learning.
- Whenever possible, work with students in less traditional environments: take field trips, use other parts of the school and the community as a place to learn.
- Have students work in teams. Students can do learning simulations, memory games, debates, drills, mind maps and dramas. (Check the lists under learning styles for more ideas.) Team learning is fun and creates a sense of cohesiveness, support and trust that can give students a sense of belonging.

- Use flip charts, graphs and mind maps as visual aids to assist students with storing information. Use colored markers for emphasis and post the information where it can be easily referred to.
- Use visualizations, word and sound associations, and role-playing to help students process and remember information.
- As soon as you see the boredom cues (kids yawning, staring out the window, doodling, note-passing, doing homework from another class), do physical energizers and play games so students can move around and get refocused. Use high energy music to reenergize the classroom.
- Play classical music (preferably baroque or chamber) softly during class. It relaxes students and puts them in a receptive state of mind for learning.
- Do relaxation exercises to reenergize and refocus the students.

A sample relaxation exercise:

- Ask students to sit comfortably either on chairs, on the floor, on pillows, etc.
- Play relaxing classical music (baroque or chamber).
- Speak softly, and **slowly** guide students through steps a to f:
  a. Close your eyes, take a deep breath and slowly let your breath out as you listen to the music.
  b. Concentrate on your body and relax each part as I speak. Feel your body respond.
  c. Begin by relaxing your scalp… then your forehead… your eyes… your cheeks… your mouth… your neck.
  d. Drop your shoulders… relax your arms… then your chest… your abdomen… your lower back… hips… thighs… knees… legs… ankles… feet… toes.

- Allow students a few quiet moments in this state. Then say:
  e. Count backward slowly from five to one and visualize yourself in a peaceful place.
- Allow students some time in their peaceful place. Then say:
  f. Count up from one to five and open your eyes when you're ready, feeling refreshed and great.

For students who experience difficulty relaxing their muscles, suggest they first tighten or clench the appropriate muscle and then release it. For example, ask them to make a tight fist and then release it by opening up their hand.

By feeling the difference between a tight muscle and a relaxed one, students may begin to sense the difference between being in a tense state and a relaxed state.

2. *Creating a Sense of Belonging in the Classroom*

"Things do not change; we change."
— Henry David Thoreau

Evaluating your teacher-student relationship style:

Is there:

- a bond that lets your students know you care?
- a positive rapport that nurtures your students' self-esteem?
- a strong peer support system in your classroom that helps students feel accepted and supported by each other?
- an emotionally safe learning environment where students can risk learning?

Students with high self-esteem:

a. are motivated.
b. are self-confident.
c. are eager to learn.
d. make friends easily.
e. are cooperative.
f. assume new responsibilities.
g. are responsible risk-takers.
h. are independent, creative and imaginative.

Students with low self-esteem:

a. have difficulty making or keeping friends.

b. feel isolated.
c. are withdrawn.
d. rarely talk in groups.
e. take very little initiative.
f. can't make decisions.
g. don't stand up for themselves.
h. constantly fear rejection and social alienation.

How to build a lasting rapport with students:

1. Be real. Be vulnerable. Share a part of yourself with your students. Be an emotionally safe person to be around. Be consistent. Answer all questions from a position of love.
2. Teach through caring, not control. Encourage your students to care about each other.
3. Use an approachable voice. Allow for genuine feedback from your students.
4. Lead by example, not fear.
5. Do and say whatever is needed to empower your students to be their best.

Class meetings:

The purpose of class meetings is:

1. To create a caring support network for students to help eliminate their feelings of isolation and rejection.
2. To develop the self-confidence in students to speak up and express themselves in a group setting.
3. To offer students the opportunity to reflect and take responsibility for their actions.
4. To create positive school experiences that motivate students to become lifelong learners.

Class meetings will guide students from feeling:

- Powerless to powerful.
- Dependent to independent.
- Vulnerable to responsible for their own feelings and for resolving their own conflicts.

Initiating the class meetings:

1. Call the group together in a non-threatening manner. Use genuine respect. Speak from your heart, using an approachable voice that allows for openness and sharing. Avoid using manipulation, fear or guilt. Students must feel safe in the group for the class meetings to work. Otherwise, little will be accomplished by holding the meetings.
2. Have students assemble comfortably in a circle or group.
3. Avoid using sharing time to reprimand students for past poor behaviors or incorrect work.
4. Start by sharing first. Allow yourself to be vulnerable. Model the behavior you would like your students to imitate.
5. Ask the students, "Who has something they would like to share with the group?" Take the time to understand their world from their point of view. Avoid "selling" them your idea of how the world works. Instead, enlarge your own world to include theirs.
6. To encourage students to participate and listen to each other, it may be helpful to pass an object from student to student. Use an object such as a microphone or a heart with "Speaking from the Heart" written on it. The student holding the object is the speaker. All the other students listen until the object is passed to them.

   Questions to help students think on deeper levels:

   a. What did you learn from the experience?
   b. How will the experience help you in the future?

7. Students often use the pronoun "you" instead of "I" when talking about themselves. They say things such as, "You know when you're afraid because you can't do something," instead of saying, "When I'm afraid because I can't do something..." As sharing time progresses and students begin to sense a connection with their feelings and actions, urge them to use the pronoun "I" to have ownership of their actions and thoughts. Do it gently, otherwise the students may think their way of talking does not meet with your approval.
8. Students may use slang while sharing, which may also include some minor swearing. To maintain the safety and non-judgmental experience of the sharing session, it's better to allow it. If the language becomes excessive, simply ask the students to restate their comments without swearing.
9. Students who don't participate should not be forced to speak. Regularly include them by asking if they have anything to share. Remember, sharing can be extremely difficult for some students.
10. When students are sharing emotionally, let them share in their own manner and give them space to be alone afterward, if needed.
11. Always thank the student for sharing and have the group also show their support by saying simple things like, "I appreciate your sharing," "I like what you said," or "That's great." At the end of the session be sure to reaffirm the love and caring you have developed for each other. Use hugs, if appropriate, or warm words of acknowledgment.
12. At the end of the school day you may want to have a class meeting in order to finish the day with a sense of solidarity. These meetings can also help you identify the needs of your students that have not been met.

Questions for the end of the day:

a. How was your day?
b. What was great? What wasn't?
c. What did you learn from each program or lesson?
d. What do you want more of?
e. What should be changed?

➤ **IMPORTANT:** During the first few meetings, sharing may be light and superficial. Allow students the time to get comfortable with the process. Once students feel safe, they will start to talk about what they feel, not just about what someone else has said.

Rules for sharing:

Rules for the sharer:

1. Be specific.
2. Use "I" statements. Speak from your own experience.

Rules for the listener:

3. Share something of yourself before asking a question.
4. Don't interrogate.
5. Don't give any fix-its, you shoulds, or advice.
6. Everything said in the sharing session is confidential and the confidentiality is forever.

➤ **IMPORTANT:** Breaking confidentiality is very serious. If confidentiality is not maintained, the sharing process will become superficial and social. The level of trust will cease to exist and will be very difficult to reestablish.

Class meetings are working when students:

- Sit closer together.
- Use supportive language.
- Share more and at deeper levels.
- Act like supportive friends.

Icebreakers:

The following are questions that may be used as icebreakers to help your students begin to share:

1. What gifts or talents were you given for which you are grateful?
2. If you were to make a bumper sticker that expresses you to the world, what would it say?
3. What makes you happy? Share one of your happiest experiences.
4. What makes you sad? Share one of your saddest experiences.
5. If you could do, have or be anything you wanted in your wildest dreams, what kind of future would you invent for yourself?
6. Describe an activity that you find personally fulfilling.
7. How do you feel about yourself at this moment in time?
8. Relate an experience of loneliness.
9. Describe a time when you really wanted to help someone but were unable to do so.
10. Share ways in which you have personally changed over the last few years. What events have changed your life?

Handling problems:

1. If your students have a complaint, resolve the problem by turning it into a win-win situation.
2. Listen non-judgmentally to what your students have to say.

Recognize that there's a problem and discover what you can agree with. Thank the students for sharing their concern and appreciate their honesty for sharing the problem with you.

3. If students feel they have been wronged, discuss the problem with them non-judgmentally, then apologize. Getting the last word is not important.
4. Ask your students if there are any other issues you need to address. If the students know they have been heard and that you care, there should be little difficulty in discovering and meeting any of their additional needs.

3. Improving Grades by Understanding Learning Styles

Most people learn best through one learning style or modality, but have enough of a balance in their other modalities that learning is not a problem. If, however, individuals have only one strong way of learning and their other modalities are weak, it may affect their ability to learn.

Identifying the auditory learner:

(Learns best by hearing information)

Usually:

- likes to talk to themselves when working – sometimes they move their lips while reading.
- enjoys reading aloud and listening to stories – often has to hear the information for it to make sense.
- spells out loud better than on paper – may not know if it looks right but can catch spelling errors by hearing if it sounds right.
- better at telling information than writing it, and can be a great speaker.
- loves to talk and discuss things.
- learns by listening, and remembers what was discussed.
- learns by associating information with sounds or words.
- likes to have instructions talked through.
- likes music better than art.
- easily distracted by noise.

- learns as if there's a tape recorder in their heads.
- learns new languages easily.

Identifying the kinesthetic learner:

(Learns best by handling information)

Usually:

- can't sit still for long periods of time – needs to move to learn.
- learns best by manipulating and doing things.
- has "messy" organizational skills.
- responds well to physical rewards.
- is a sensitive, intuitive person who judges situations by feelings.
- touches people to get their attention and stands close to them when they're talking.
- uses a finger as a pointer when reading.
- gestures a lot.
- memorizes by walking, talking, seeing and doing.
- talks slowly and uses action words.
- has messy handwriting.
- likes to act things out.
- likes games and action books.
- learns best from hands-on experiences.
- is physically oriented and can't remember geography unless the place has been visited.
- works better in a comfortable, non-stressful environment.
- doesn't care what the teacher knows, unless they know the teacher cares.

Identifying the visual learner:

(Learns best by seeing information)

Usually:

- is neat, orderly and organized.

- is a good long-range planner.
- is a good speller and can mentally visualize the words.
- is observant of details – remembers what is seen rather than what is heard.
- memorizes best by mentally creating visual pictures of the information to be remembered.
- speaks quickly.
- is not distracted by noise.
- has trouble remembering verbal instructions and often asks to have them repeated.
- is a strong fast reader who would rather read alone than be read to.
- would rather do a demonstration than make a speech.
- likes art more than music.
- knows what to say but can't think of the right words.
- tunes out even when intending to pay attention.
- answers with a simple 'yes' or 'no.'
- doodles during telephone conversations and meetings.
- forgets to relay verbal messages.
- needs to see the big picture and know the overall purpose before proceeding on a lesson or project.
- has to see you in order to hear you.

Classroom activities for different learning styles:

Classroom lessons and activities should take into account and try to accommodate all of the students' senses. Students strong in only one modality need to develop their other senses.

Many of the activities in each of the following categories will accommodate more than one style of learning.

AUDITORY ACTIVITIES

debates
dramas
lectures
commercials
interviews
plays
singing
puppet plays
talking books
travelogues
panel discussions
talk about it
riddle/joke-telling
court case trials
telephone conversations
television shows
choral reading
quiz shows
student teaches lesson
demonstrations
workshops
song writing
making audio tapes
oral reports
radio broadcasts
choral speaking
storytelling
role-playing
reader's theater
speeches
use of language master
slide-, film-, video-presentations

KINESTHETIC ACTIVITIES

shadow plays
experiments
sculpture
model making
dancing
role-playing
workshops
displays
inventions
acting
measuring
flip books
scrolls
scrapbooks
documentaries
plasticine
computers
interest kits
stitchery
carving
puppet plays
costumes
game simulations
mimes
videos
plays
repairing
painting
collages
bumper stickers
surveys
codes
flannel board stories
board games
mobiles
masks
terrariums
trips
puzzles
roving storyteller
demonstrations
interest centers
television shows
building
cut and paste
murals
bulletin boards
animation
tracing
games
quizzes

VISUAL ACTIVITIES		
advertisements	photo essays	diagrams
flow charts	calendars	poetry corner
sketches	charts	coloring books
tables	illustrations	films
critiques	filmstrips	graphs
maps	picture storybooks	newspaper articles
time-lines	cartoons	overheads
posters	want ads	blueprints
paintings	handbooks	stories
novels	summaries	comic strips
letters	menus	editorials
book covers	reports	questionnaires
worksheets	task cards	recipes
documents	lists	research
brochures	biographies	booklets
pamphlets	telegrams	epitaphs
proverbs	wills and testaments	photos
journals	diaries	logbooks
display tables	collections	mind maps

reviews of books, theater, movies
writing comics, short stories, cartoons, how-to books, educational books

Study strategies for students:

It's important for students to be aware of which study strategies will work best for their style of learning. Changing their study habits may improve their performance and increase their grades.

Study strategies for the auditory learner:

1. Talk to yourself, go over ideas and information out loud. Explain it to someone. Teach it to yourself or get a study buddy to discuss the material with you. Form a study group.

2. Don't play music or have the television on when you're studying. You can be easily distracted by any kind of noise.
3. If possible, tape lectures and replay them. Remember to make word or sound associations with the details you want to remember.
4. When you've been assigned work, repeat the instructions back to your teacher to make sure they're clear.
5. When studying, sing the information or make up rhymes to help you remember.
6. To get information, use television or radio news programs. If you have the opportunity, give oral reports.
7. Learn to spell by using phonics. Practice spelling words out loud. When you're not sure how to spell a word, repeat the letters out loud to find the error.
8. If you're having problems comprehending a written passage, read it out loud.
9. You have a good memory for discussions and learn by listening, so pay attention in class. It will help improve your grades.
10. To memorize, do it in steps. Talk to yourself.

Study strategies for the kinesthetic learner:

1. Touch and handle things. Build, manipulate and repair things.
2. Keep moving. A good way to learn something is to walk and talk about it.
3. Use diagrams, mind maps and models. Make your own study charts to organize information and details. Use different colors when charting information to help you remember the facts.
4. Use a notebook to keep track of assignments.
5. Study buddies are a good idea. Act out information and role-

play. Use lots of gestures to explain the information.

6. Practice your spelling by looking at the words while tracing them in the air with your finger or your nose.
7. Point to the words when reading; it will help your comprehension.
8. Get involved in projects, experiments, making models, making videos, role-playing and acting. Use your physical senses. Do things out loud. Use a hands-on approach to learning.
9. Use typewriters, calculators, computers.
10. Take lots of breaks. Snack while studying.

Study strategies for the visual learner:

School is designed for these learners. If they pay attention in class, do all their assignments and study for tests, they usually do well and have few problems in school.

1. Use visual cues or visual associations to remember details.
2. Put notes in places to help you remember.
3. Take notes in class. Review them, and then summarize them.
4. Use color-coded mind maps, charts, graphs, diagrams and pictures to help you remember information and capture important ideas.
5. Use highlighter pens in different colors when reading to point out important information.
6. For information, read newspapers, books, magazines. Go to the library.
7. Do written reports. You're good at them.
8. Memorize by seeing pictures of the information in your mind.
9. Practice spelling by seeing the words in your mind.
10. In college, take advantage of the smaller tutorial groups, especially if you find it difficult to learn in large lecture halls.

Everyone is a combination, in varying degrees, of all the senses or modalities. Some of the strategies for one modality may apply to you even if it's not your strongest sense. If you have a strategy, and it's not listed here but works for you, continue using it.

To develop your weaker modalities or learning styles, visual learners should practice reciting out loud and adding body movement to their learning. Auditory learners should practice visualizing information as well as adding movement to their learning. Kinesthetic learners should practice picturing information in their minds and reciting it out loud.

4. *How to Set Goals*

"Destiny is not a matter of chance, it is a matter of choice. It is not a thing to be waited for, it is a thing to be achieved."
— William Bryan Jennings

To go from feeling powerless to powerful:

1. Plan for your success.
2. Know what your goals are and how you're going to achieve them.
3. Learn to measure your own progress against your own aims and objectives.
4. Look back over your progress and acknowledge, "Yes, I've done that," and "Yes, I can do more."

Action plan:

1. Make a list of the areas of your life in which you are not happy. The list may include your personal life, relationships, academic progress, career, finances or any other area you want to plan for.
2. Write down individual goals for each area. Word each goal as an action and include the time within which you're committed to accomplishing these goals, such as: one week, one month, six months, two years. Be very specific.

   For example:

   - I will save $50 a week to buy a car by March of next year.
   - I will take weekly Spanish lessons and will be able to converse in Spanish by the end of this year.

- I will read one science book per month of at least 200 pages for the next six months.
- I will practice the piano for one hour every day for the next year.
- I will study history for one hour each night for the next three months.

Make sure you direct your goals toward things you can affect. Your goals should not be dependent on other people changing. The outcome must be in your control.

3. Then write down what your life will be like when you've achieved your goals. List the reasons why you're committed to making each goal a reality within the given time limit. Include what you will be like and how your life will be better. What will you see, hear and feel in your external world? If you can't answer these questions, you will not know when you have achieved your goals.
4. Write down what your life will be like if you don't achieve your goals.
5. Then write down the step-by-step actions necessary to achieve each goal. Define each action and sub-action needed to get you where you want to go.
6. Make a list of the important resources you already have and those you still need. Then find out how to get the resources you're missing. Ask yourself: What do I need to do that I haven't already done? Whom do I need to meet that I haven't already met? Knowledge helps to create the confidence that you're taking the best route available to reach your goals.
7. Find a mentor, if possible someone who has already achieved what you want. Watch and analyze this person's success. Copy it.
8. Include evaluation dates that state when you will review your goals. At these times look objectively at your plan and make any necessary adjustments. Review your goals regularly, at least once a month or more. This helps to keep you on track.

➤ **IMPORTANT:** Writing goals that aren't specific or don't have a set date for completion may mean you haven't made a conscious commitment to achieving them. If you're making excuses as to why you can't, instead of realizing why you can, you may never get past dreaming about how life could be.

Guidelines for setting goals:

Goals need to be:

1. Something you believe in.
2. Something you really want to be, do or have.
3. Measurable in time.
4. Stated clearly.
5. Non-destructive to oneself or to others.

Tips for making it:

- Keep a logbook of your progress.
- Look for feedback. Correct when you're off course.
- There is no such thing as failure, only opportunities for learning.

5. Creating Positive Student Evaluations

"Nothing would be done at all if you waited until you could do it so well that no one could find fault in it."
— Cardinal Newman

Student report cards should offer constructive information with regard to the academic goals and objectives set out by the students in consultation with their teacher. Reports should encourage students to improve their skills and inspire them to become lifelong learners.

The benefits of student self-evaluations:

1. Encourages students to scrutinize their own work indepth.
2. Sharpens their analytical and critical thinking skills.
3. Improves their ability to evaluate and monitor their own progress.
4. Offers students an opportunity to show their different thinking skills.
5. Improves their performance.
6. Develops an atmosphere of trust between the teacher and student, and reduces the student's fear of failure.
7. Helps students develop more confidence in expressing their own ideas.
8. Offers teachers valuable insights into what motivates and interests their students.
9. Offers teachers the opportunity to modify their role and be seen as more approachable, as a helper rather than as a judge.

Suggestions for initiating self-evaluation:

1. Supply students with clearly defined criteria.
2. Brainstorm with students to find a method of evaluation that students feel comfortable with.
3. Define some criteria and leave some evaluations open-ended.

Questions to consider when:

A. Discussing students' organization and planning:

- How did you choose your working space?
- How have you organized this project?
- Why did you choose to organize in this manner?
- Are you having any problems with the assigned task?
- How might you do it differently? More efficiently?
- Have you planned enough time to complete your assignment?
- How long do you expect it to take before the assignment is completed?
- Do you need more information?
- How would you prefer to present the information?
- Are you working with anyone? How are you sharing the responsibilities? How did you divide up the work? Who is the leader of the group and how was it decided?

B. Discussing the results of students' work:

- What new ideas did you come up with for this project?
- What roadblocks did you run into?
- How might you have done it differently?
- What could you have done better?
- What did you learn that you didn't know before?
- What did you have to research?
- How could this information affect your life?

- What would you like to learn about in the future?

C. Discussing student relationships:

- What do you like to do with your friends?
- What do you need to establish a level of trust with another person?
- Do you allow others to know how you feel? How might you let them be more aware of your needs?
- What creates respect in you for another person? What do you do to gain the respect of others?
- How do you feel about yourself?
- What are your interests outside of school?
- What are you planning to do when you finish school?
- What could you do to take more responsibility for your life?
- How are you feeling about...? How might that have been handled differently? How do you think the other person felt? How would you have felt?

APPENDIX B

Associations for Parents and Educators

A parent is a child's first and most important teacher.

For those of you who wish to get involved in making a difference in your children's/students' lives, this section lists many of the parent and educational organizations that are working toward that goal. The list contains many associations which offer information and help on specific educational issues. Many of the addresses given are for the national offices. If your regional office is not listed, please contact the national office for your local chapter. *This list is not exhaustive and is* **not** *an endorsement of any of the organizations; it is merely a reference section of educational associations.*

To be considered for a listing in future editions or to update current entries, organizations should contact: Bayhampton Publications, PMB 264, 2900 Delk Road, Suite 700, Marietta, GA 30067-5320; phone: (905) 455-7331; fax: (905) 455-0207; e-mail: Bayhampton@aol.com.

UNITED STATES ASSOCIATIONS

DROPOUT PREVENTION:

Aspira Association, Inc.
National Office
1444 Eye Street, NW
Washington, DC 20005
(202) 835-3600

Big Brothers/Big Sisters of America
230 North 13th Street
Philadelphia, PA 19107
(215) 567-7000

Boys and Girls Clubs of America
1230 West Peachtree Street, NW
Atlanta, GA 30309
(404) 487-4700 or (800) 854-CLUB

Communities in School, Inc
1199 North Fairfax, Suite 300
Alexandria, VA 22314-1436
(703) 519-8999

Girls Incorporated
120 Wall Street, 3rd Floor
New York, NY 10005-3902
(212) 509-2000

National Dropout Prevention Center
Clemson University
209 Martin Street
Clemson, SC 29631-1555
(864) 656-2599 or (800) 443-6392

EDUCATIONAL ASSOCIATIONS:

American Association of School Administrators
1801 North Moore Street
Arlington, VA 22209-1813
(703) 528-0700

American Forum for Global Education
120 Wall Street, Suite 2600
New York, NY 10005
(212) 624-1300

American Indian Institute
College of Continuing Education
University of Oklahoma
555 Constitution, Suite 237
Norman, OK 73072-7820
(405) 325-4127 or (800) 522-0772

American School Counselor Association
801 North Fairfax Street, Suite 310
Alexandria, VA 22314
(703) 683-2722 or (800) 306-4722

Appalachia Educational Laboratory, Inc.
P.O. Box 1348
1031 Quarrier Street
Charleston, WV 25325-1348
(304) 347-0400 or (800) 624-9120

Associates for Renewal in Education, Inc.
45 P Street, NW
Washington, DC 20001
(202) 483-9424

Association for Community Based Education
1805 Florida Avenue, NW
Washington, DC 20009
(202) 462-6333

Association for Effective Schools, Inc.
44 Sharptown Road
Stuyvesant, NY 12173
(518) 758-9828

Association for Experiential Education
2305 Canyon Blvd., Suite 100
Boulder, CO 80302
(303) 440-8844

Center for Educational Renewal
313 Miller Hall, Box 353600
University of Washington
Seattle, WA 98195-3600
(206) 543-6230

Center for Research on the Education of Students Placed at Risk
Holy Cross Hall, Room 427
2900 Van Ness Street, NW
Washington, DC 20008
(202) 806-8484

Center for School Change
234 Humphrey Center
301 19th Avenue South
Minneapolis, MN 55455
(612) 626-1834

Center for Social Organization of Schools
Johns Hopkins University
3003 North Charles Street, Suite 200
Baltimore, MD 21218
(410) 516-8800

Center for the Study of Small/Rural Schools
University of Oklahoma
555 East Constitution Street, #211
Norman, OK 73072-7820
(405) 325-1450 or (800) 937-4760

Coalition of Essential Schools
1814 Franklin Street, Suite 700
Oakland, CA 94612
(510) 433-1451

Consortium for School Networking
1555 Connecticut Avenue, NW, Suite 200
Washington, DC 20036
(202) 466-6296

Creative Education Foundation
1050 Union Road, Suite 4
Buffalo, NY 14224
(716) 675-3181

Indiana Education Network, Inc.
803 East 46th Street
Indianapolis, IN 46226
(317) 543-3318

Institute for Independent Education
1313 North Capitol Street, NE
Washington, DC 20002
(202) 745-0500

Intercultural Development Research Association
5835 Callaghan Road, Suite 350
San Antonio, TX 78228-1190
(210) 444-1710

Mid-Continent Regional Educational Laboratory
2550 South Parker Road, Suite 500
Aurora, CO 80014
(303) 632-5552 or (800) 949-6387

National Association for the Education of Young Children
1509 16th Street, NW
Washington, DC 20036-1426
(202) 232-8777 or (800) 424-2460

National Association of Elementary School Principals
1615 Duke Street
Alexandria, VA 22314-3483
(703) 684-3345 or (800) 386-2377

National Association of Independent Schools
1620 L Street, NW, Suite 1100
Washington, DC 20036
(202) 973-9700

National Association of Partners in Education, Inc.
901 North Pitt Street, Suite 320
Alexandria, VA 22314
(703) 836-4880 or (800) 992-6787

National Black Child Development Institute
1023 15th Street, NW, Suite 600
Washington, DC 20005
(202) 387-1281 or (800) 556-2234

National Catholic Educational Association
1077 30th Street, NW, Suite 100
Washington, DC 20007-3852
(202) 337-6232

National Education Association
1201 16th Street, NW
Washington, DC 20036-3290
(202) 822-7350

National Head Start Association
1651 Prince Street
Alexandria, VA 22314
(703) 739-0875 or (800) 687-5044

National Rural Education Association
Colorado State University
246 Education Building
Fort Collins, CO 80523-1588
(970) 491-7022

National Society for Experiential Education
1703 North Beauregard Street
Alexandria, VA 22311-1714
(703) 575-5475

North Central Regional Educational Laboratory
1900 Spring Road, Suite 300
Oak Brook, IL 60523
(630) 571-4700 or (800) 356-2735

Northwest Regional Educational Laboratory
101 Southwest Main Street, Suite 500
Portland, OR 97204-3297
(503) 275-9500 or (800) 547-6339

Reading is Fundamental, Inc.
600 Maryland Avenue, SW, Suite 600
Washington, DC 20024
(202) 287-3220 or (877) 743-7323

Research for Better Schools, Inc.
444 North Third Street
Philadelphia, PA 19123-4107
(215) 574-9300

Southern Early Childhood Association
7107 West 12th Street, Suite 102
Little Rock, AR 72204
(501) 663-0353 or (800) 305-7322

Southwest Educational Development Laboratory
211 East 7th Street
Austin, TX 78701-3281
(512) 476-6861 or (800) 476-6861

Wave, Inc.
525 School Street, SW, Suite 500
Washington, DC 20024
(202) 484-0103 or (800) 274-2005

EDUCATIONAL INFORMATION:

Educational Information and Resource Center
Research Department
606 Delsea Drive
Sewell, NJ 08080
(609) 582-7000

Eric Clearinghouse on Elementary and Early Childhood Education
University of Illinois at Urbana-Champaign
Children's Research Center
51 Gerty Drive
Champaign, IL 61820-7429
(217) 333-1386 or (800) 583-4135

Eric Clearinghouse on Higher Education
The George Washington University
One Dupont Circle, NW, Suite 630
Washington, DC 20036-1183
(202) 296-2597 or (800) 773-3742

Eric Clearinghouse on Rural Education and Small Schools
Appalachia Educational Laboratory
1031 Quarrier Street, Suite 607
P.O. Box 1348
Charleston, WV 25325-1348
(304) 347-0400 or (800) 624-9120

Eric Clearinghouse on Teaching and Teacher Education
American Association of Colleges for Teacher Education
1307 New York Avenue, Suite 300
Washington, DC 20005-4701
(202) 293-2450 or (800) 822-9229

Eric Clearinghouse on Urban Education
Columbia University Teachers College
Institute for Urban and Minority Education
Main Hall, Room 303, P.O. Box 40
New York, NY 10027-6696
(212) 678-3433 or (800) 601-4868

Global Learning, Inc.
1018 Stuyvesant Avenue
Union, NJ 07083-6023
(908) 964-1114

LaBriola National American Indian Data Center
University Libraries
P.O. Box 871006
Arizona State University
Tempe, AZ 85287-1006
(480) 965-0270

Synergy Learning, Inc.
116 Birge Street, #3
P.O. Box 60
Brattleboro, VT 05302-0060
(802) 257-2629 or (800) 769-6199

HOME SCHOOLING:

Alliance for Parental Involvement in Education
P.O. Box 59
East Chatham, NY 12060-0059
(518) 392-6900

National Center for Home Education
P.O. Box 3000
Purcellville, VA 20134
(540) 338-7600

National Coalition of Alternative Community Schools
1266 Rosewood, Unit 1
Ann Arbor, MI 48104-6205
(734) 668-917

Parents as Teachers National Center, Inc.
10176 Corporate Square Drive, Suite 230
St. Louis, MO 63132
(314) 432-4330

PARENT ASSOCIATIONS:

Asociacion de Padres Pro Bienestar de Ninos Impedidios de Puerto Rico, Inc.
P.O. Box 21301
Ponce de Leon #724 Altos
Hato Rey, PR 00918
(787) 763-4665 or (800) 981-8393

Children's Defense Fund
25 E Street, NW
Washington, DC 20001
(202) 628-8787 or (800)233-1200

Chandler Education Foundation, Inc.
1527 West Frye Road
Chandler, AZ 85224-2006
(480) 812-7632

Connects
Geneseo Migrant Center, Inc.
27 Lackawanna Avenue
Mt. Morris, NY 14510
(716) 658-7960 or (800) 245-5681

Delaware Parent Education Resource Center Child, Inc.
507 Philadelphia Pike
Wilmington, DE 19809-2177
(302) 762-8989 or (800) 874-2070

Family Advocate Program, Inc.
P.O. Box 8808
Boise, ID 83707-2808
(208) 345-3344 or (800) 574-7544

Family Resource Center Coalition
Nebraska SPRING Project
Blue Valley Community Action, Inc.
6949 South 110th Street
Omaha, NE 68128
(402) 597-4831 or (888) 550-3722

Family Resource Coalition
20 North Wacker Drive, Suite 1100
Chicago, IL 60606
(312) 338-0900

Family Works
Child Care Connection, Inc.
8300 Colesville Road, Suite 700
Silver Spring, MD 20910
(301) 608-8173 or (877) 937-3639

Families United for Success
Life Service System of Ottawa County, Inc.
160 South Waverly Road
Holland, MI 49423
(616) 396-7566 or (800) 577-7661

Iowa Parent Information Resource Center
The Higher Plain, Inc.
1025 Penkridge Drive
Iowa City, IA 52246
(319) 354-5606

Keys for Networking, Inc.
117 Southwest Sixth Avenue
Topeka, KS 66603-3805
(785) 233-8732 or (800) 499-8732

National Community Education Association
3929 Old Lee Highway, Suite 91-A
Fairfax, VA 22030
(703) 359-8973

National Family Partnership
2490 Coral Way, Suite 301
Miami, FL 33145-3449
(305) 856-4173 or (800) 705-8997

National PTA – National Congress of Parents and Teachers
330 North Wabash Avenue, Suite 2100
Chicago, IL 60611-3690
(312) 670-6782 or (888) 425-5537

National Parent to Parent Support and Information System, Inc.
P.O. Box 907
Blue Ridge, GA 30513
(706) 374-3826 or (800) 651-1151

National Urban League
120 Wall Street, 8th Floor
New York, NY 10005
(212) 558-5300

Native American Parental Assistance Program
Ahmium Education, Inc.
P.O. Box 366
San Jacinto, CA 92581-0366
(909) 654-2781 or (888) 217-2242

Parent Advocacy Coalition for Educational Rights, Inc.
4826 Chicago Avenue South
Minneapolis, MN 55417-1098
(612) 827-2966 or (800) 53-PACER

Rhode Island Parent Information Network, Inc.
175 Main Street
Pawtucket, RI 02860
(401) 727-4144 or (800) 464-3399

Sanctuary, Inc.
P.O. Box 21030, GMF
Barrigada, GU 96921
(671) 475-7103

SPECIAL EDUCATION ASSOCIATIONS (Disabilities and Gifted):

American Association for Gifted Children
Duke University
Box 90270
Durham, NC 27708-0270
(919) 783-6152

American Association on Mental Retardation
444 North Capitol Street, NW, Suite 846
Washington, DC 20001-1512
(202) 387-1968 or (800) 424-3688

Center for Innovations in Special Education
Parkade Center, Suite 152
601 Business Loop 70 West
Columbia, MO 65211
(573) 884-7275 or (800) 976-CISE

Center on Human Policy
Syracuse University
805 South Crouse Avenue
Syracuse, NY 13244-2280
(315) 443-3851 or (800) 894-0826

Connecticut Parent Advocacy Center, Inc.
338 Main Street
Niantic, CT 06357
(860) 793-3089 or (800) 445-2722

Council for Exceptional Children
Divisions for: Children with Behavioral Disorders
Early Childhood
Mental Retardation and Developmental Disabilities
Visual Handicaps
Gifted
Learning Disabilities
1920 Association Drive
Reston, VA 22091-1589
(703) 620-3660 or (888) 232-7733

Council for Learning Disabilities
P.O. Box 40303
Overland Park, KS 66204
(913) 492-8755

Disability Rights Education and Defense Fund, Inc.
2212 Sixth Street
Berkeley, CA 94710
(510) 644-2555 or (800) 466-4232

Eric Clearinghouse on Disabilities and Gifted Education
Council for Exceptional Children
1920 Association Drive
Reston, VA 22091-1589
(800) 328-0272

Gifted Development Center
1452 Marion Street
Denver, CO 80218
(303) 837-8378 or (888) 443-8331

Idaho Parents Unlimited, Inc.
Parent Education Resource Project Center
4696 Overland Road, Suite 568
Boise, ID 83705
(208) 342-5884 or (800) 242-4785

Learning Disabilities Association of America
4156 Library Road
Pittsburgh, PA 15234-1349
(412) 341-1515 or (888) 300-6710

Mentor Parent Program Inc.
P.O. Box 47
Pittsfield, PA 16340
(814) 563-3470 or (888) 447-1431

National Association for Gifted Children
1707 L Street, NW, Suite 550
Washington, DC 20036
(202) 785-4268

National Association for Visually Handicapped
22 West 21st Street
New York, NY 10010
(212) 889-3141

National Association of Private Schools for Exceptional Children
1522 K Street, NW, Suite 1032
Washington, DC 20005
(202) 408-3338

National Center for Learning Disabilities
381 Park Avenue South, Suite 1401
New York, NY 10016
(212) 545-7510 or (888) 575-7373

National Information Center for Children and Youth with Disabilities
P.O. Box 1492
Washington, DC 20013-1492
(202) 884-8200 or (800) 695-0285

Parents, Inc.
4743 East Northern Lights Boulevard
Anchorage, AK 99508
(907) 337-7678 or (800) 478-7678

Parent Education Project of Wisconsin, Inc.
2192 South 60th Street
West Allis, WI 53219-1568
(414) 328-5520 or (800) 231-8382

Parents Helping Parents, Inc.
3041 Olcott Street
Santa Clara, CA 95054-3222
(408) 727-5775

Partners Resource Network, Inc.
Path Project
1090 Longfellow, Suite B
Beaumont, TX 77706-4819
(409) 898-4684 or (800) 866-4726

Peak Parent Center, Inc.
6055 Lehman Drive, Suite 101
Colorado Springs, CO 80918
(719) 531-9400 or (800) 284-0251

Resources for Children with Special Needs, Inc.
200 Park Avenue South, Suite 816
New York, NY 10003
(212) 677-4650

Special Education Action Committee, Inc.
P.O. Box 161274
Mobile, AL 36616-2274
(334) 478-1208 or (800) 222-7322

Western Regional Resource Center
1268 University of Oregon
Eugene, OR 97403-1268
(541) 346-5641

SUBSTANCE ABUSE:

American Council for Drug Education
164 West 74th Street
New York, NY 10023
(212) 595-5810 or (800) 488-3784

American Council on Alcoholism, Inc.
3900 North Fairfax Drive
Arlington, VA 22203
(703) 248-9005

Council on Alcohol and Drugs, Inc.
2045 Peachtree Road NE, Suite 605
Atlanta, GA 30309
(404) 351-2840

Drug Information and Strategy Clearinghouse
P.O. Box 8577
Silver Spring, MD 20907
(800) 955-2232

National Association of Substance Abuse Trainers and Educators, Inc.
1521 Hillary Street
New Orleans, LA 70118
(504) 286-5000

National Clearinghouse for Alcohol and Drug Information
P.O. Box 2345
Rockville, MD 20847-2345
(301) 468-2600 or (800) 729-6686

National Families in Action
Century Plaza II
2957 Clairmont Road, Suite 150
Atlanta, GA 30329
(404) 248-9676

Safer Society Foundation
P.O. Box 340
Brandon, VT 05733-0340
(802) 247-3132

VIOLENCE IN EDUCATION:

Advocates for Justice and Education, Inc.
2041 Martin Luther King Jr. Avenue, SE, Suite 301
Washington, DC 20020
(202) 678-8060 or (888) 327-8060

Juvenile Justice Clearinghouse
Box 6000
Rockville, MD 20849-6000
(800) 638-8736

National Center for the Study of Corporal Punishment and Alternatives
Temple University
Ritter Hall Annex 253
Philadelphia, PA 19122
(215) 204-6091

National School Safety Center
141 Duesenberg Drive, Suite 11
Westlake Village, CA 91362
(805) 373-9977

CANADIAN ASSOCIATIONS (by Province)

ALBERTA:

Alberta Home and School Association (AHSCA)
607, 11010-142nd Street
Edmonton, Alberta, T5N 2R1
(403) 454-9867

Calgary Association for Effective Education of the Learning Disabled
Site 2, S.S.3, P.O. Box 103
Calgary, Alberta, T3C 3N9
(403) 686-6444

Calgary Society for Students with Learning Difficulties
3930-20th Street S.W.
Calgary, Alberta, T3C 3N9
(403) 686-6444

Learning Disabilities Association of Alberta
145, 11343-61st Avenue.
Edmonton, Alberta, T6H 1M3
(780) 448-0360

BRITISH COLUMBIA:

Delta Association for Handicapped Children
3, 3800-72nd Street
Delta, British Columbia, V4K 1M2
(604) 946-6622

International Dyslexia Association - BC
#523-409 Granville Street
Vancouver, BC V6C 1T2
(604) 669-5811

Learning Disabilities Association of British Columbia
1524 Fort Street
Victoria, BC V8S 5J2
(250) 370-9513

Native Education Center
285 East 5th Avenue
Vancouver, British Columbia, V5T 1H2
(604) 873-3761

Surrey Association for Early Childhood Education
6225B-136th Street
Surrey, British Columbia, V3X 1H3
(604) 597-3200

MANITOBA:

Learning Disabilities Association of Manitoba
60 Maryland Street, 2nd Floor
Winnipeg, Manitoba, R3G 1K7
(204) 774-1821

NEW BRUNSWICK:

Learning Disabilities Association of New Brunswick
88 Prospect Street West
Fredericton, New Brunswick, E3B 2T8
(506) 459-7852

NEWFOUNDLAND:

Learning Disabilities Association of Newfoundland and Labrador
P.O. Box 26036
St. John's, Newfoundland, A1B 3T1
(709) 754-3665

NOVA SCOTIA:

Learning Disabilities Association of Nova Scotia
1800 Argyle Street, Suite 517
Halifax, Nova Scotia, B3T 3N8
(902) 423-2850

NORTHWEST TERRITORIES:

Learning Disabilities Association of the Northwest Territories
P.O. Box 242
Yellowknife, Northwest Territories, X1A 2N2
(867) 873-6378

ONTARIO:

Association of Early Childhood Educators
40 Orchard View Boulevard, Suite 217
Toronto, Ontario, M4R 1B9
(416) 487-3157

Association of Parent Support Groups of Ontario
P.O. Box 27581
Yorkdale Postal Outlet
Toronto, Ontario, M6A 3B6
(416) 223-7444

Big Brothers of Canada
3228 South Service Road
Burlington, Ontario, L7N 3H8
(905) 639-0461

Boys and Girls Clubs of Canada
7100 Woodbine Avenue
Unionville, Ontario, L3R 5J2
(905) 477-7272

Canadian Alliance of Home Schoolers
272 Highway #5, RR 1
St. George, Ontario, N0E 1N0
(519) 448-4001

Canadian Council for Exceptional Children
1010 Polytek Court, Unit 36
Gloucester, ON K1L 9J2
(613) 747-9226

Canadian Education Association
252 Bloor Street West, Suite 8-200
Toronto, Ontario, M5S 1V5
(416) 924-7721

Canadian Institute of Child Health
885 Meadowlands Drive, Suite 512
Ottawa, ON K2C 3N2
(613) 224-4144

Head Injury Association
45 Sheppard Avenue East, Suite 419
Toronto, Ontario, M2N 5W9
(416) 222-1911

Learning Disabilities Association of Canada
200-323 Chapel Street
Ottawa, Ontario, K1N 7Z2
(613) 238-5721

Learning Disabilities Association of Ontario
365 Bloor Street East
Toronto, Ontario, M4W 3L4
(416) 929-4311

National Education Association of Disabled Students
Unicentre, Room 426
Carleton University
Ottawa, ON K1S 5B6
(613) 526-8008

Ontario Association for Bright Children
2 Bloor Street West, Suite 100-156
Toronto, Ontario, M4W 2G7
(416) 925-6136

Ontario Federation of Home and School Associations
1240 Bay Street
Toronto, Ontario, M5R 2A7
(416) 924-7491

PRINCE EDWARD ISLAND:

Learning Disabilities Association of P.E.I.
P.O. Box 1081, Station Main
Charlottetown, Prince Edward Island, C1A 7M4
(902) 892-4137

QUEBEC:

Quebec Learning Disabilities Association
284 Notre Dame Street West, Suite 300
Montreal, Quebec, H2Y 1T7
(514) 847-1234

SASKATCHEWAN:

Learning Disabilities Association of Saskatchewan
Alberta Community Centre
26-610 Clarence Avenue
Saskatoon, Saskatchewan, S7H 2E2
(306) 652-4114

AUSTRALIAN ASSOCIATIONS

A.C.T. Council of Parents and Citizens Associations
Majura Primary School
Knox Street, Watson
ACT 2602
(06) 241-5759

Australian Parents Council Inc.
P.O. Box 1894
North Sydney
New South Wales 2059
(02) 955-7091

Concerned Parents Association
P.O. Box 1041
Geelong
Victoria 3220

Federation of Parents and Citizens Association of New South Wales
210 Crown St.
Sydney
New South Wales 2010
(02) 360-2481

Isolated Children Parents Association
Private Mail Bag 10
Cobar
New South Wales 2835
(068) 81-2264

Isolated Childrens Parents Association - Queensland Council
Jabinda
Tambo
Queensland 4478
(076) 546-257

Parents and Friends' Federation of Western Australia Inc.
P.O. Box 222
Wembley
Western Australia 6014
(09) 387-5377

Queensland Council of Parents and Citizens Associations
P.O. Box 370
Stones Corner
Queensland 4120
(07) 391-0988

Victorian Federation of State School Parents Clubs Inc.
Town Hall,
Queensbury Street
North Melbourne
Victoria 3051
(03) 328-4380

BRITISH ASSOCIATIONS

Campaign for State Education (CASE)
158 Durham Road
London, England, SW20 0DG
0181-9448206

Greater London Federation of Parent-Teacher Associations
20 Airlie Gardens
Ilford, England, 1G1 4LB

Home and School Council
40 Sunningdale Mount
Sheffield, England, S11 9HA
0114-2364181

National Autistic Society
276 Willesden Lane
London, England, NW2 5RB
0181-451-1114

National Confederation of Parent-Teacher Associations
2 Ebbsfleet Industrial East
Stonebridge Road
Gravesend,
Kent, England, DA11 9DZ
01474-560618

National Council for Special Education
Exhall Grange
Wheelwright Lane
Coventry, England, CV7 9HP
01203-352414

National Education Association
1 Hinchley Way
Hinchley Wood, Esher
Surrey, England, KT10 0BD
0181-3981253

INTERNATIONAL ASSOCIATIONS

Association for Childhood Education International
17904 Georgia Avenue, Suite 215
Olney, MD 20832-2277
(301) 570-2111 or (800) 423-3563

International Alliance for Learning
P.O. Box 26175
Colorado Springs, CO 80936
(719) 596-6827 or (800) 426-2989

International Dyslexia Association
Chester Building
8600 LaSalle Road, Suite 382
Baltimore, MD 21286-2044
(410) 296-0232

NAFSA: Association of International Educators
1307 New York Avenue, NW, 8th Floor
Washington, DC 20005-4701
(202) 737-3699

Bibliography and Suggested Reading

COMMUNICATION:

Buntman, Peter H. and Eleanor M. Saris, *How to Live with your Teenager*. U.S.A.: The Birch Tree Press, 1988.

Buscaglia, Leo, *Love*. Canada: Fawcett Crest, 1985.

Gelb, Michael J., *Present Yourself*. CA: Jalmar Press, 1988.

Gibb, Jack, *Trust*. CA: Guild of Tutors Press, 1978.

Jeffers, Susan, Ph.D., *Feel the Fear and Do It Anyway*. New York: Fawcett Columbine, 1987.

Laborde, G.Z., *Influencing with Integrity*. CA: Syntony Publishing, 1983.

Vasey, Paul, *Kids in the Jail*. Canada: Black Moss Press, 1995.

LEARNING STYLES:

Butler, Kathleen A., Ph.D., *It's All in Your Mind: A Student's Guide to Learning Style*. Columbia, CT: The Learner's Dimension, 1988.

Gregoric, Anthony, *An Adult's Guide to Style*. Maynard, MA: Gabriel Systems, 1982.

Keefe, J.W., *Learning Style Theory and Practice*. Reston, VA: NASSP, 1987.

National Association of Secondary School Principals, *Student Learning Styles – Diagnosing and Prescribing Programs*. Reston, VA: NASSP, 1979.

Silvernail, D., *Teaching Styles as Related to Student Achievement: What Research Says to the Teacher.* Washington, DC: National Education Association, 1979.

Tobias, Cynthia U., *The Way We Learn*. Colorado Springs, CO: Focus on the Family, 1994.

SELF-ESTEEM:

Branden, Nathaniel, Ph.D., *The Power of Self-Esteem*. Deerfield, FL: Health Communications Inc., 1992.

Canfield, Jack, *Self-Esteem in the Classroom*. CA: Self-Esteem Seminars, 1990.

Pollard, John K., *Self-Parenting*. Malibu, CA: Generic Human Studies Publishing, 1987.

Robbins, Anthony, *Unlimited Power*. U.S.A.: Fawcett Columbine, 1986.

Robbins, Anthony, *Awaken the Giant Within*. New York: Summit Books, 1991.

Vegotsky, Ken, *The Ultimate Power*. Los Angeles: Ages Publications, 1995.

TEACHING STRATEGIES:
*(information on learning styles is included in books marked with *)*

Bills, Robert E., *Education for Intelligence or Failure?* Washington, DC: Acropolis Books, 1982.

Buzan, Tony, *The Mind Map Book – Radiant Thinking*. London, England: BBC Books, 1993.

Byham, William C., Ph.D., *Zapp in Education*. New York: Fawcett Columbine, 1992.

Dennison, Paul E., Ph.D. and Gail E. Dennison, *Brain Gym*. Glendale, CA: Edu-Kinesthetics, 1986.

*DePorter, Bobbi, *Quantum Learning*. New York: Dell Publishing, 1992.

*Dryden, Gordon and Jeannette Vos, Ph.D., *The Learning Revolution*. CA: Jalmar Press, 1994.

Glasser, William, M.D., *Schools Without Failure*. New York: Harper and Row, 1969.

*Grinder, Michael, *Righting the Educational Conveyor Belt*. U.S.A.: Metamorphous Press, 1989.

Holt, John, *How Children Fail.* New York: Dell, 1964.

Illich, Ivan, *Deschooling Society*. New York: Harper and Row, 1970.

*Jensen, Eric P., *Super-Teaching*. U.S.A.: Turning Point, 1988.

Kline, Peter, *The Everyday Genius*. Arlington, VA: Great Ocean Publishers, 1988.

Lieberman, Laurence, *Preventing Special Education.* MA: GloWorm, 1984.

Lipsky, Dorothy K., Ph.D. and Alan Gartner, Ph.D. (eds.), *Separate Education*. Baltimore, MD: Paul H. Brookes Publishing Co., 1989.

Maslow, Abraham H., *Motivation and Personality*. New York: Harper, 1954.

Messick, S. and Associates., *Individuality in Learning*. San Francisco: Jossey-Bass, 1976.

Ohme, Herman, *Learn How to Learn*. CA: California Education Plan, Inc., 1986.

Ostrander, Sheila and Lynn Schroeder, *Super-Learning*. New York: Dell, 1982.

Putnam, JoAnne W. (ed.), *Cooperative Learning and Strategies for Inclusion*. Baltimore, MD: Paul H. Brookes Publishing Co., 1993.

Rose, Colin, *Accelerated Learning*. U.S.A.: Dell, 1987.

Rosenthal, R. and L. Jacobson, *Pygmalion in the Classroom*. New York: Holt, Rinehart and Winston, 1968.

Wycoff, Joyce, *Mindmapping*. New York: The Berkley Publishing Group, 1991.

References

Alves, A. and Gottlieb, J. Teacher interactions with mainstreamed handicapped students and their non-handicapped peers. *Learning Disability Quarterly, 9*, 77-83, 1986.

Baumeister, R.F. and Leary, M.R. The need to belong: Desire for interpersonal attachments as a fundamental motivation. *Psychology Today*, *117*(3) 497-529, 1995.

Brophy, J.E. *Research on self-fulfilling prophecy and teacher expectation*. Paper presented at the annual meeting of the American Educational Research Association, New York, 1982.

Byrne, D.B., Hattie, J.A. and Fraser B.J. Students perceptions of preferred classroom learning environments. *Journal of Educational Research, 80*(1) 10-18, 1986.

Caslyn, R.J. The causal relation between self-concept, locus of control, and achievement: A cross lagged panel analysis. (Doctoral dissertation, Northwestern University, 1973). *Dissertation Abstracts International, 42*, 4076a, 1974.

Coombs, R.H. and Harper, J.L. Effects of labels on attitudes of educators toward handicapped children. *Exceptional Children, 33*, 399-403, 1967.

Cooter, S. Why you didn't learn and how you can. *Journal of the Society for Accelerative Learning and Teaching, 6*(3), 212-236, 1981.

Danner, F.W. and Lonky, E. A cognitive-development approach to the effects of rewards on intrinsic motivation. *Child Development, 52*, 1043-1052, 1981.

Deci, E.L. Effects of externally mediated rewards on intrinsic motivation. *Journal of Personality and Social Psychology, 18*, 105-115, 1971.

Deci, E.L. and Ryan, R.M. The empirical exploration of intrinsic motivational processes. In L. Berkowitz (Ed.), *Advances in experimental social psychology (Vol. 13)*. 39-80. New York: Academic Press, 1980.

deGroat, A.F. and Thompson, G.G. A study of the distribution of teacher approval and disapproval among sixth grade pupils. *Journal of Experimental Education, 18*, 57-75, 1949.

Dunn, R.S. and Dunn, K.J. Learning styles/teaching styles. Should they... can they... be matched? *Educational Leadership, 36*(4), 238-244, 1979.

Edmonds, R. Some schools work and more can. *Social Policy, 9*(2), 28-32, 1979.

Ellison, L. What does the brain have to do with learning? Even most educators don't know! *Holistic Education Review*, Fall, 41-45, 1990.

Felix, U. Students' attitudes toward the use of music and mind-calming in their high school language class. *Journal of the Society for Accelerative Learning and Teaching, 12*(3&4), 141-167, 1986.

Foster, G.G. Schmidt, C.R. and Sabatino, D. Teacher expectancies and the label "learning disabilities." *Journal of Learning Disabilities, 9*, 58-61, 1976.

Good, T.L. Classroom expectations: Teacher-pupil interactions. In J. McMillan (Ed.), *The Social Psychology of School Learning*. New York: Academic Press, 1980.

Gregorac, A.F. Learning/teaching styles: Potent forces behind them. *Educational Leadership, 36*, 234-36, 1979.

Gregoric, A.F. Style as a symptom: A phenomenological perspective. *Theory into Practice, 23*(1), 51-55, 1984.

Haertel, G.D., Walberg, H.J. and Haertel, E.H. Socio-psychological environments and learning: A quantitative synthesis. *British Educational Research Journal, 7, 27-36,* 1981.

Harter, S. The perceived competence scale for children. *Child Development, 53*, 87-97, 1982.

Held, D. Case study: Now Johnny can read. *Journal of the Society for Accelerative Learning and Teaching, 4*(3), 170-176, 1979.

Held, D.F. *The Intuitive Approach to Reading and Learning Disabilities*: A practical alternative. Springfield, Ill: Charles C. Thomas, 1984.

Hogan, P. *A Community of Teacher Researchers: A Story of Empowerment and Voice*. Unpublished manuscript, University of Calgary, 1988.

Hoge, R.D. and McSheffrey, R. An investigation of self-concept in gifted children. *Exceptional Children, 57*(3), 238-245, 1991.

Hughes, M. Using the means of suggestion to harmonize with the barriers. *Journal of the Society for Accelerative Learning and Teaching, 7*(1), 70-81, 1982.

Johnson, D.W., Maruyama, G., Johnson, R., Nelson, D. and Skon, L. Effects of cooperative, competitive, and individualistic goal structures on achievement: Ameta-analysis. *Psychological Bulletin, 89*, 47-62, 1981.

Lipsky, D.K. and Gartner, A. Capable of achievement and worthy of respect: Education for handicapped students as if they were full-fledged human beings. *Exceptional Children, 54*(1), 69-73, 1987.

Lortie, D. Some reflections on renegotiation. In M. Reynolds (Ed.), *Futures of Education for Exceptional Students* (pp. 235-244). Reston VA: The Council for Exceptional Children, 1978.

Lozanov, G. The suggestological theory of communication and instruction. *Suggestology and Suggestopedia, 1*(3), 1-13, 1975

Lozanov, G. and Balevski, P. The effect of the suggestopedic system of instruction on the physical development, state of health and working capacity of first and second grade pupils. *Suggestology and Suggestopedia, 1*(3), 24-32, 1975.

Marshall, J. Making sense as a personal process. In P. Reason and J. Rowan (Eds.), *Human Inquiry: A Sourcebook of New Paradigm Research*. New York: John Wiley &Sons, 1981.

Meyer, L.H. and Henry, L.A. Cooperative classroom management. In J.W. Putnam (Ed.), *Cooperative Learning and Strategies for Inclusion*. (pp. 93-121). Baltimore, MD: Paul H. Brookes Publishing Co., 1992.

Miller, A. Love: Unspoken catalyst of suggestopedia. *Journal of the Society for Accelerative Learning and Teaching, 10*(4), 253-259, 1985.

Pallak, S.R., Costomiris, S., Sroka, S. and Pittman, T.S. School experience, reward characteristics, and intrinsic motivation. *Child Development, 53*, 1382-1391, 1982.

Pariser, E. Intimacy, connectedness, and education. *Holistic Education Review*,Winter, 4-9, 1990.

Parker, I., Gottlieb, B.W., Gottlieb, J., Davis, S. and Kunzweiller, C. Teacher behavior toward low achievers, average achievers, and mainstreamed minority group learning disabled students. *Learning Disabilities Research, 4*(2), 101-106, 1989.

Potterbaum, S.M., Keith, T.Z. and Ehly, S.W. Is there a causal relation between self-concept and academic achievement? *Journal of Educational Research, 79*(3),140-144, 1986.

Pratton, J. and Hales, L.W. The effects of active participation on student learning. *Journal of Educational Research, 79*(4), 210-215, 1986.

Raviv, A., Raviv, A. and Reisel, E. Teachers and students: Two different perspectives? Measuring social climate in the classroom. *American Educational Research Journal, 27*(1), 141-157, 1990.

Salomon, G. and Perkins, D.N. Rocky road to transfer: Rethinking mechanisms of a neglected phenomenon. *Educational Psychologist, 24*(2), 113-142, 1989.

Sims, P. An exploration of students' experiences with the learning program supercamp. Unpublished Masters project, Brock University, St. Catharines, ON, 1991.

Stanton, H.E. Facilitating learning through the building of morale. *Journal of the Society for Accelerative Learning and Teaching,* 6(1), 59-63, 1981.

Stanton, H.E. Ego-state reframing: One possible answer to school problems. *Journal of the Society for Accelerative Learning and Teaching,* 9(2), 157-164, 1984.

Stanton, H.E. Creating happiness: The use of submodalities. *Australian Journal of Adult Education, 28,* 3-6, 1988.

Stoddard, L. Developing geniuses, how to stop the great brain robbery. *Holistic Education Review*, Spring, 28-33, 1991.

Story, N.O. and Sullivan, H.J. Factors that influence continuing motivation. *Journal of Educational Research, 80*(2), 6-92, 1986.

Summer, L. Tuning up the classroom with music and relaxation. *Journal of the Society for Accelerated Learning and Teaching,* 6(1), 46-50, 1981.

Valle, J.D., Dunn, K., Dunn, R., Geisert, G., Sinatra, R. and Zenhausern, R. The effects of matching and mismatching students' mobility preferences on recognition and memory tasks. *Journal of Educational Research,* 79(5), 267-272, 1986.

Vos-Groenendal, J. An accelerated/learning model program (ALMP) based on participants' perceptions on attitude and achievement. Unpublished doctoral dissertation, Northern Arizona University, Flagstaff, Arizona, 1991.

Wang, M., Haertel, G.D. and Walberg, H.J. What influences learning? A content analysis of review literature. *Journal of Educational Research, 84*(1), 30-43, 1990.

Webb, G.M. Left/right brains, teammates in learning. *Exceptional Children, 1*(1),238, 1983.

Weisz, J.R. and Stipek, D.J. Competence, contingency, the development of perceived control. *Human Development, 25,* 250-281, 1982.

Ysseldyke, J.E., Algozzine, B., Richey, L. and Graden, J. Declaring students eligible for learning disabilities services: Why bother with the data? *Learning Disability Quarterly,* 5(1), 37-44, 1982.

Index

T

V

W

About the Author

Pamela Sims, M.Ed., is an educational motivator and consultant. She has been an educator for over twenty years and is a specialist in Special Education, with a Master's degree in Educational Administration. She speaks internationally at conferences and conducts seminars and workshops for parents, educators and students on relationship building, empowerment, self-worth and learning skills.

Dear Reader, Meeting Planner and Speakers Bureau:

Pamela Sims, M.Ed. can make your next convention, conference or professional development day an uplifting, memorable experience. Engage her as your keynote speaker, seminar or workshop facilitator.

Here's what Educators, Seminar Participants and Parents are saying about Pamela's workshops and consultations...

"Few trainers have both the educational background and real-world skill level Pamela enjoys. Her ability to demonstrate what she's teaching makes her training effective, motivational and fun. I'm glad I attended this training."

John Rainforth, Ph.D., Counselor

"Your seminar offered us fantastic ways to enhance ourselves as individuals and educators. It was powerful and practical."

Normand Deslandes, Speaker and Life Coach

"Terrific, Inspiring, Great Experience, were just a few of the words I heard at our retreat. The group was brought together in a short period of time, allowing the remainder of the week-end for sharing and growth."

Mary Kay Kurzweg, Speaker and Facilitator

"By far the best seminar I've ever attended. It takes a lot to impress me and I was impressed."

Aldo Malatesta, Teacher

"It is without reservation that I would recommend Pamela Sims."

Patricia J. Dawson, Assistant Head, Student Affairs

"Your session was inspirational, informative, entertaining and upbeat. It made us all feel valued for the job we do."

Sandy Mitchell, Principal

"We wish every teacher could have been there to bring your message of caring back to the classroom."

Jane Hersey, National Director, FAUS

"It helped me to see that I have to be in touch with myself, so that I can be supportive to students. Really puts our teaching careers in perspective."

Dianne Moore, Maine Support Network

"The teachers loved your excellent presentation. It was inspiring, well-paced, informative and fun."

Lorri Moffatt, Staff Development

"Very positive. Related well to what teachers are experiencing today."

Ruth Marcille-Smith, Teacher

Programs available:

- Awakening Your Brilliance
- Awakening Children's/Students' Potential
- Is it a Behavior Problem or a Learning Problem?
- Building Self-Esteem through Trust, Love and Communication in the Classroom

Customized programs available on request.

To arrange a presentation for your school or organization, contact:

Pamela Sims, M.Ed. & Associates
PMB 264, 2900 Delk Road, Suite 700
Marietta, GA 30067-5320
Phone: (905) 455-7331; Fax: (905) 455-0207
E-mail: Pksims@aol.com; www.Pamelasims.com